# THE FAIRTRADE
## EVERYDAY COOKBOOK

# THE FAIRTRADE

# EVERYDAY COOKBOOK

Consultant Editor  Sophie Grigson

DK

LONDON, NEW YORK, MELBOURNE, MUNICH, AND DELHI

Editor Constance Novis
Photographic Art Direction and Design Miranda Harvey
Photographer William Reavell
Food Stylist Amanda Wright
Prop Stylist Victoria Allen

Project Art Editor Caroline de Souza
Managing Editor Dawn Henderson
Managing Art Editor Heather McCarry
Editorial Assistant Ariane Durkin
Production Editor Jenny Woodcock
Production Controller Sarah Sherlock

First published in Great Britain in 2008
by Dorling Kindersley Limited
80 Strand, London WC2R 0RL

Penguin Group (UK)

A CIP catalogue record for this book is available from The British Library

ISBN: 978 1 4053 2005 4

Colour reproduction by MDP, UK
Printed and bound in Hong Kong by Sheck Wah Tong Printing Press Ltd.

Discover more at
www.dk.com

# CONTENTS

## FILL ME UP! 22

Chicken and Apricot • Spicy Cashew Nut Soup • Jean's One-Pot Chicken • Fruit and Nut Pilaff • Creamy Bacon Pasta with Roasted Vegetables • Grilled Ginger Salmon with Oriental Spicy Rice • Go Go Chicken • **Sarah Randell** Lamb Shanks with Tomatoes, Honey, Cinnamon, and Saffron • Green Banana Curry • **Producer** Cuban Orange Chicken • Spiced Potato Patties • **Sheherazade Goldsmith** Richard's Sweet and Sour Pork Ribs • Quinoa with Moroccan Sauce • Chicken Mole • North African Chicken • **Noel McMeel** Fillet of Beef with Champ and Gravy • Mushroom Stroganoff • **Joanne Harris** Lamb Tagine • **Sir Steve Redgrave** Baked Penne with Dolcelatte Cheese and Radicchio • Thai Fish Curry • **Sophie Grigson** Slow-Roast Shoulder of Pork with Quinces or Apples • Chicken Pie • **Eileen Maybin** Beef, Mango, and Celery in Red Wine • Cheesy Rice Balls in Tomato Sauce • Fair-ly Fruity Coconut Curry • Fruity North African Salad • Roast Lemon-Herb Chicken • **George Alagiah** Fragrant Rice • Orange-Coated Chicken with Mango • Vegetable Biryani

## I MUST HAVE SOMETHING SWEET RIGHT NOW! 64

Microwave Choccy Bikkies • Chocolate Chip Brownies • Fruity Jelly • Orange and Chocolate Puddings • Rose and Vanilla Ice Cream • Apricot and Cherry Loaf • Spiced Bars • A Fair Banana Loaf • Banana and Chocolate Muffins • Pear and Chocolate Cake • Marma-Banana Crunchies • Chocolate and Beetroot Little Fancies • **Producer** Indian Spiced Vanilla Chai • Chocolate, Cherry, and Coconut Slice • Fruit and Nut Flip-Flaps • Anzac Biscuits • Apple and Sultana Cake • Toffee Brownies • Chocolate Orange Tealoaf • Banana and Nut Fingers • Apricot Muffins • Taste of the Caribbean Banana Bread • Nutty "Drop" Buns • Apricot and Oat Squares • Sticky Banana Fingers • Smooth Oasis • Rich Chocolate and Coconut Pudding • **Rose Gray and Ruth Rogers** Espresso and Hazelnut Cake • The Ultimate Energy Bars • Takes the Biscuit! • Banana, Walnut, and Orange Loaf • Sticky Banoffee Muffins • Trinidadian Coconut Sweetbread • Banana and Date Loaf • Raspberry Flapjacks • Chocolate Brazil Banana Bread • Fairtrade Cookies • Fruity Loaf • Mango and Brazil Nut Teabread • Teabread • Simple Mango Sorbet • Chocolate and Ginger Cookies • Irish Teacake • Wholemeal Fruitcake • Huxley Hedgehog Biscuits • Fruity Apple Cake

## LIGHT BITES 120

Rice and Corn Cakes with Spicy Prawns • Secret Soup • **Allegra McEvedy** Superfoods Salad • Chicken, Apricot, and Almond Rice • **Producer** Malawian Peanut Futali • Green Tea Chicken with Lemon Rice • Piquant Prawn and Pineapple Pilaff • **Oz Clarke** Salmon Koulibiaca • Winter Salad • **Antony Worrall Thompson** Prawn and Mango Ceviche • Tropical Chicken Salad • **Hugh Fearnley-Whittingstall** Kedgeree • Summer Prawn and Mango Noodle Salad • Japanese-style Duck Breasts with Aromatic Rice • **Producer** Caribbean Banana Salad • Mango, Avocado, and Brown Rice Salad • **Natasha Kaplinsky** Summer Salad • **Adjoa Andoh** Tilapia Fish and Rice • Vegetable, Ginger, and Pineapple Chilli Stew • Peppered Salmon

## GUILTY PLEASURES 156

Busy Day Mocha Banana Cake • Honey and Coconut Cookies • Spiced Pineapple Cake • Chocolate and Chestnut Tureen • Cookie Feast Pizza • Easy-Make Tropical Banana Cake • Grandma's Chocolate Chunk Ginger Biscuits • Rich Dundee Cake • Indulgent but Easy Peasy Pudding • Icky Sticky Toffee Pudding • Rocky Road Brownies • Honey Cake • Lavender Ice Cream • Mango Yoghurt Brûlées • Fruit and Crisp • Banana Butterscotch Pudding • White Chocolate Cakes • Banana Crumble Cake • Scrummy Crumble • Rich Mocha Cake • Chocolate Apple Cake • Mango and Pineapple Pavlova • Chocolate Mousse • Drizzled Banana Sunshine Surprise • Fairtrade Tiffin • Chocolate Cherry Bites • Knickerbocker Glory • Pofesen • Bitter Chocolate, Apricot, and Almond Tart • Strawberry Meringue Stack • Gluten-free Chocolate Cake • Triple Chocolate Bars • Coffeetime Muffins • White Chocolate Cheesecake • Pannacotta with Port Sauce • Chocolate Fudge Cake • **Producer** Indian Basmati Rice Pudding • Pineapple Upside-Down Cake • Sunshine Rice Pudding • Tropical Spiced Pineapple • Banana Rhumba • Dark Chocolate Fondant • Quick Rum Bananas • Fair and Passionate Pineapple Dessert with Grown-up Chocolate Buttons

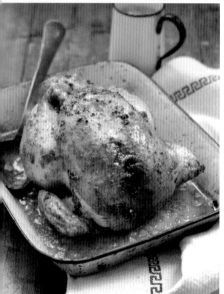

# RECIPE NAVIGATOR

The recipe navigator is organized by the main ingredient in the dish, so you can see all of the recipes at a glance. If you fancy a dessert using pineapple, for example, have a look through the navigator.

# FOREWORD

The Fairtrade movement has come a long, long way in the past few decades. It's spreading and growing and drawing in more producers and, as importantly, more consumers. Here, amongst all the doom and gloom we are surrounded by, is a positive beacon of hope. Buying Fairtrade ingredients is a small way to make a big difference.

Not only do you and I get something good to cook with and eat or drink, but someone else, the person who put in all the work growing or making that item, gets a decent wage. In short, a win-win situation. Naturally in a reasonable and right-thinking world this would be standard practice, and indeed many shoppers in the UK assume that it is. It comes as something of a shock to discover that this perfectly fair assumption is often wrong.

This is why the FAIRTRADE Mark is so important. It's your guarantee that the spices, or chocolate or wine or rice that you've slipped into your shopping basket have been produced and traded honestly and fairly. The range of Fairtrade goods is ever-growing. Where once it was dominated by coffee, tea, and chocolate, now it includes dried fruits, spices, fresh fruit and vegetables, nuts, jams and chutneys, biscuits, yoghurt, and much more. And that's just the edible stuff...

In the pages of this book you will find recipes that have been contributed by a few of the burgeoning community of people who include Fairtrade ingredients in their daily diets. I've tasted my way through a generous selection with considerable satisfaction, so I know that you will derive great pleasure from delving amongst them and establishing your own personal favourites, safe in the knowledge that you are making the world a better place.

Sophie Grigson

# INTRODUCTION

## by the Fairtrade Foundation

The inspiration for this recipe book came from the mountain of imaginative recipes using Fairtrade ingredients that members of the public have been sending the Fairtrade Foundation over the years. As the number of recipes has grown, so has the range of products and the awareness of the positive impact of choosing Fairtrade.

To find some of the country's favourite original recipes made with Fairtrade ingredients, the Fairtrade Foundation teamed up with publisher Dorling Kindersley to launch a competition during Fairtrade Fortnight 2007, the annual two-week awareness-raising campaign held in March. People were invited to send in their own recipes, featuring a Fairtrade product as the main ingredient or flavouring, or using as many Fairtrade products as possible. Celebrities who support Fairtrade also contributed their recipes.

Guarantees a **better deal** for Third World Producers

FAIRTRADE

® Firm favourites, such as banana loaf and chocolate brownies, featured heavily in the entries but many people experimented with less well-known Fairtrade products such as lavender sugar, wine, and vanilla pods. And that was the exact purpose of the competition – to get people cooking across the range of Fairtrade products. The diversity gave the judging panel, made up of food writer Sophie Grigson, Sarah Randell, Food Director at *Sainsbury's Magazine*, and Eileen Maybin, Media Relations Manager at the Fairtrade Foundation, a great spread of dishes to taste and test. The winning recipes are featured in this book alongside contributions from some of the farmers and workers' communities who supply Fairtrade products. With 59 developing countries worldwide and

*Look out for the FAIRTRADE Mark whenever you shop.*

over seven million people – farmers, workers, and their families – benefiting from Fairtrade, it really is a global movement of producers and consumers making trade fairer together.

## What is Fairtrade?

For most of us, sitting down with family or friends to enjoy a home-cooked meal is one of life's great pleasures. In the UK we can choose from a huge variety of exciting ingredients, including fresh fruit from the Caribbean and Africa, tea, rice, and spices from Asia, and coffee, cocoa, and sugar from Central America. Yet, for the communities growing such food, life is often far from sweet. At the mercy of volatile or declining global commodity prices and unfair trading practices, many farmers and workers struggle to provide their families with basics such as clean water, schooling, and healthcare. But Fairtrade puts the power of trade back into the hands of the farmer and worker by offering:

*Aquilino Duran is a banana farmer in the Dominican Republic who has benefited from Fairtrade.*

• fair and stable prices that cover the cost of sustainable production.

• an extra payment, called a Fairtrade premium, which producers can invest in projects of their choosing to improve their future, such as building roads and health clinics, or improving water, or local school provision.

• pre-financing of contracts to provide cash flow without the need for costly loans.

• longer-term trading relationships so people can plan and budget for the future.

## Fairtrade Farmers

Jennipher Wettaka is a coffee farmer and member of the Gumutindo Coffee Co-op in Uganda. Her farm is in the Mbale district of eastern Uganda, on the lower slopes of Mount Elgon, where the rich volcanic soil, warm climate, and plentiful rainfall make the area ideal for growing high-quality Arabica coffee.

Before Gumutindo was established, women like Jennipher had to carry the heavy sacks of coffee to villages up to 10 kilometres (6 miles) away to sell to local traders. They would have to take whatever price was offered or carry the coffee all the way back to their farms. Now, 85 per cent of Gumutindo's coffee is sold to Fairtrade buyers. This means the co-op can predict their income for the year and plan future community projects, such as building more classrooms and improving the road infrastructure.

Aquilino Duran, a banana farmer in the Dominican Republic, receives an agreed and stable price from Fairtrade sales, which can be around a dollar a box more than he would earn from the conventional market. In addition, the co-op of which he is a member, ASOBANU, receives a Fairtrade premium for every

*Look out for tea and biscuits that carry the FAIRTRADE Mark.*

box of bananas sold. Aquilino says, "We have used the premium to establish projects in the community, such as improvements to schools, house repairs, and healthcare. And we've invested it in sports facilities for young people because sport helps them keep out of trouble."

## How can you support Fairtrade?

By choosing Fairtrade products, (see www.fairtrade.org.uk) we play our part in enabling farmers and workers to bring about change today in their own lives

*Why not take part in an event or hold your own? The Fairtrade Foundation can offer you free resources with ideas for events, and kits to decorate them.*

and communities, as well as sending out a signal for justice in wider international trade. If you want to get more involved in campaigning for Fairtrade apart from eating, drinking, and wearing it, there are many ways to become a supporter. The Fairtrade Foundation runs a number of campaigns to get people involved all over the country.

Fairtrade Fortnight is a two-week awareness-raising promotion that runs every year. Thousands of events are held nationwide, from tea dances to tastings, and fashion shows to food fairs, and this provides a great opportunity to get involved. Why not take part in an event or hold your own? The Fairtrade Foundation can offer you free resources with ideas for events, and kits to decorate them, along with merchandise to promote the message to choose Fairtrade. To find out more, visit **www.fairtrade.org.uk**.

*Fairtrade chocolate is available in a wide range of tempting varieties.*

All year round, there are campaigns in schools, universities, local councils, workplaces, and communities, organized by

Fairtrade supporters to raise awareness. You could join a group representing your interests and work towards gaining Fairtrade status through such campaigns by promoting Fairtrade products. If there is not one in your area, you can set up your own group. For more information, visit www.fairtrade.org.uk/getinvolved.

## Fairtrade and trade justice

Fairtrade changes the lives of producers who are suffering as a result of unjust international trade. When we choose Fairtrade, it not only benefits producers, but also sends a message to government and business that we want to see global trade rules work better for poor people, especially in developing countries, and also for the planet. By offering farmers an agreed and stable price for their product, Fairtrade is enabling farmers' organizations not only to

*When we choose Fairtrade, it not only helps producers, but sends a message to government and business that we want to see global rules work better for poor people.*

survive, but to invest in their communities and their future. However, the reform of international trade is also required to deliver sustainable development, so the Fairtrade movement is also involved in campaigns calling on governments to enshrine justice in international trade. Many organisations, including the Fairtrade Foundation, have joined the Trade Justice Movement (TJM). For the latest information and news on campaign actions, visit www.tjm.org.uk.

"The carefully planned involvement of Fairtrade stakeholders – producers, traders, buyers, and campaigners – shows the future of Fairtrade is very promising for increasing the chances of small producers to sell more through the Fairtrade movement."
*Silver Kasoro-Atwoki, Mabale Growers Tea Factory, Uganda*

*There is a different Fairtrade fruit to enjoy every day of the week.*

# CHAPTER ONE

FILL ME UP!

# CHICKEN AND APRICOT

## INGREDIENTS

Serves 4
Preparation time 10 minutes
Cooking time 45 minutes
4 chicken breasts
2 tbsp plain flour
1 tbsp olive oil
10g (¼oz) butter

1 onion, finely chopped
1 bulb fennel, thinly sliced
50g (1¾oz) Fairtrade dried apricots (do
   not soak)
150ml (5fl oz) Fairtrade white wine
150ml (5fl oz) hot chicken stock
salt and Fairtrade black pepper

## METHOD

**Sprinkle** the flour on a plate and roll the chicken in the flour until it is coated.

**Heat** the olive oil and butter in a large deep frying pan. Add the chicken breasts and cook them for about 10 minutes, turning occasionally, until golden browned.

**Add** the onion, fennel, and apricots, and cook for 2–3 minutes until well coated. Pour in the white wine and stock. Bring everything up to the boil, then reduce the heat, cover, and simmer for about 30 minutes, until the chicken and fennel are tender and cooked through.

*Tip* You can serve the chicken with Fairtrade brown rice, cooked according to the instructions on the packet, accompanied by a seasonal vegetable, such as tenderstem broccoli. You could also use chicken thigh fillets, skinned and boned, as an alternative to the chicken breasts.

**Mrs J F Canning** from Backwell, Bristol

# SPICY CASHEW NUT SOUP

## INGREDIENTS

Serves 4
Preparation time 10 minutes
Cooking time 15 minutes

200g (7oz) Fairtrade cashew nuts
2 tablespoons vegetable or groundnut oil
1 large onion, chopped

2 cloves garlic, chopped
2 teaspoons garam masala
1 teaspoon Fairtrade ground ginger
1 litre (1¾pints) vegetable stock
Small bunch fresh coriander, chopped

## METHOD

**Grind** the cashew nuts in a food processor or chopper. Place the oil in a saucepan over a medium heat and add the chopped onion and garlic.

**Cook** gently for 2–3 minutes. Add the spices and cook for 3 minutes. Add the stock and ground cashew nuts, and simmer for about 5 minutes. Leave to cool.

**Blend** the soup with a hand blender or in a food processor until nearly smooth. Take out a couple of tablespoons of the slightly nutty mixture. Blend again until very smooth. Add the retained spoonfuls. Gently reheat the soup.

**Sprinkle** the coriander onto the soup before serving.

# TASTES LIKE A LOVELY MILD KORMA AND A SPANISH ALMOND SOUP

**Rebecca Linton** from Leicester

# JEAN'S ONE-POT CHICKEN

## INGREDIENTS

Serves 4
Preparation time 10 minutes
Cooking time 25 minutes

1 tbsp olive oil
1 leek, roughly chopped
4 skinless and boneless chicken breasts
  weighing 600g (1lb 5oz), cut into strips
2 cloves garlic, finely crushed
250g (9oz) Fairtrade basmati rice

750ml (1 ¼pints) hot chicken stock
400g (14oz) tin chopped tomatoes
1 tsp Fairtrade turmeric
½tsp Fairtrade black peppercorns,
  finely ground
200g (7oz) organic green beans,
  blanched and cut into 4cm (1½in)
  pieces
Salt

## METHOD

**Heat** the oil in a large saucepan and fry the leeks until they are tender.

**Add** the chicken strips and brown them for 4–5 minutes.

**Stir** in the garlic and rice and cook for 1–2 minutes before pouring in the stock and chopped tomatoes.

**Add** the turmeric, ground pepper, and salt and bring to simmering. Simmer gently, for around 10 minutes, until the rice is almost tender.

**Stir** in the beans, cook for 5 minutes, then taste to check the seasoning.

**Serve** and enjoy!

*Tip* For variety, you could make this recipe using bone-in chicken thigh pieces.

**Judges' note** You might like to add soy sauce or chilli sauce to finish, or serve it with garlicky yoghurt.

# WARMING AND WHOLESOME, QUICK AND SATISFYING

**Debbie Davidson** from Addlestone, Kent

# FRUIT AND NUT PILAFF

## INGREDIENTS

Serves 4
Preparation time 10 minutes
Cooking time: 20-25 minutes

2 tbsp olive oil
1 medium onion, finely chopped
2 tsp ground coriander
50g (1¾oz) Fairtrade brazil nuts, roughly chopped
50g (1¾oz) walnuts, roughly chopped

225g (8oz) Fairtrade white basmati rice, rinsed
350g (12oz) sweet potato, peeled and cut into small cubes
50g (1¾oz) Fairtrade dried apricots, quartered
750ml (1¼pints) hot vegetable stock
Salt and Fairtrade black pepper to taste
Several sprigs fresh coriander to garnish

## METHOD

Heat the oil in a large frying pan with a lid. Add the onion and fry gently for 5 minutes.

Add the ground coriander and cook for 2 minutes.

Add the nuts and rice, and stir well to give a good coating of oil. Cook for 3 minutes.

Add the sweet potato and apricots, stir, and add the hot stock.

Bring to the boil and cover. Let simmer for 12-15 minutes until the potato is tender and the stock has been absorbed.

Add seasoning to taste.

Place in a heated dish and garnish with sprigs of coriander to serve.

*Tip* Serve this with a green salad.

Judges' note If you want to, you could top this with a handful of chopped coriander, as well as a squeeze of Fairtrade lemon or lime juice, and even add in a chopped chilli. Serve with wedges of Fairtrade limes or lemons.

**Anita Ballin** from Penzance

# CREAMY BACON PASTA WITH ROASTED VEGETABLES

## INGREDIENTS

Serves 4
Preparation time 15 minutes
Cooking time 30 minutes

1 red onion, roughly chopped
3 Fairtrade peppers (mixed colours),
 roughly chopped
4 portabellini mushrooms, sliced
Handful of fresh basil leaves, torn

1 tbsp olive oil
12 vine cherry tomatoes, halved
175g (6oz) streaky bacon, chopped
500g (1lb 2oz) dried *conchiglie rigate*
 pasta shells
150g (5½oz) Emmental cheese, finely
 grated
150g (5æ½oz) half-fat crème fraîche
Fairtrade black pepper

## METHOD

**Preheat** the oven to 180°C/350°F/Gas Mark 4.

**Arrange** the onion, peppers, and mushrooms in a large roasting tray. Season, and sprinkle with the basil. Pour over the olive oil and shake to coat well.

**Place** in the oven and cook for 15 minutes. Then gently stir in the cherry tomatoes and scatter the bacon on top.

**Return** the tray to the oven and cook for another 15 minutes until the bacon is crispy and the vegetables tender.

**Cook** the pasta in a large pan of boiling water until it is al dente, following the pack instructions.

**Drain** the cooked pasta, place it in a large bowl, and fold in the cheese and crème fraiche.

**Divide** the pasta into four warmed dishes, spoon over the roasted vegetables and bacon, and sprinkle with black pepper.

*Tip* This rich recipe will serve four generously. If you like, you can garnish the finished dish with a few chopped fresh basil leaves.

**Mrs F E Wyman** from Cornwall

# GRILLED GINGER SALMON WITH ORIENTAL SPICY RICE

## INGREDIENTS

Serves 4
Preparation time 10 minutes
Cooking time 25 minutes

4 fillets salmon, skin on, weighing
approximately 150g (5½oz) each
2 tbsp olive oil, plus extra for brushing
1 tsp Fairtrade ground ginger
2 large onions, finely chopped

2 garlic cloves, finely crushed
100g (3½oz) Fairtrade raisins
1 cinnamon stick
1 tsp Fairtrade ground turmeric
3 Fairtrade cloves
300g (10oz) Fairtrade basmati rice
A few fresh chives, to garnish

## METHOD

**Place** the salmon on a foil-lined grill rack. Brush the fillets with olive oil, sprinkle them with ground ginger, and set aside. Fill the kettle and put it on to boil.

**Heat** the remaining olive oil gently in a large deep frying pan. Add the onion and garlic and cook for 4–5 minutes until soft and golden.

**Stir** in the raisins, cinnamon stick, turmeric, and cloves, and cook for 3–4 minutes.

**Add** the rice and about 600ml (1 generous pint) boiling water to cover. Bring to simmering, cover, and cook gently for 15–20 minutes or until the rice is tender. Then remove the cinnamon stick and cloves, drain the rice, and keep it warm.

**Preheat** the grill to 200°C/400°F/Gas Mark 6 towards the end of the rice cooking time. When the grill is hot, cook the salmon fillets for 5 minutes on each side until the flesh starts to flake. Serve each fillet on a bed of rice garnished with the chives.

**Judges' note** Stir-fried greens tossed with a little fresh ginger and chilli would make a delicious accompaniment to this dish.

**Ruth Dan** from Worcester Park, Surrey

# GO GO CHICKEN

## INGREDIENTS

Serves 4
Preparation time 10 minutes
Cooking time 12 minutes

200g (7oz) organic couscous
2 tbsp olive oil
1 medium onion, finely chopped
1 Fairtrade red pepper, sliced
1 green chilli, deseeded and finely
  chopped

4 skinless chicken breasts, sliced
1 Fairtrade mango, peeled, stone
  removed, and diced
1 Fairtrade lemon, zest and juice
Half of a 15g (½oz) pack fresh coriander,
  roughly chopped
Salt and Fairtrade black pepper
25g (1oz) Fairtrade cashew nuts,
  chopped, to serve

## METHOD

**Place** the couscous in a large bowl or pan and add 275ml (9fl oz) boiling water. Cover and set aside for 10 minutes.

**Heat** 1 tbsp of the oil in a large frying pan meanwhile, and cook the onion, pepper, and chilli for 1–2 minutes until fragrant. Then add the chicken and stir constantly for 8–10 minutes until it is thoroughly cooked.

**Stir** in the mango and heat for 1 minute.

**Drizzle** the rest of the oil into the couscous and stir in the zest and juice of the lemon and the chopped coriander. Season well.

**Pile** the couscous onto warm plates and top with the chicken and mango mix.

**Sprinkle** with cashew nuts to serve.

**Judges' note** This is so easy to make and quick, it would be a terrific dish to serve to an unexpected guest.

**Sam Miller** from St Alban's, Hertfordshire

# LAMB SHANKS WITH TOMATOES, HONEY, CINNAMON, AND SAFFRON

## Sarah Randell

At Sainsbury's Magazine we are keen supporters of Fairtrade. This recipe requires several Fairtrade ingredients, and it freezes well too. You can serve it with Fairtrade basmati rice, tossed with slivers of toasted almonds and freshly chopped flat-leaf parsley.

## INGREDIENTS

Serves 4

4 tbsp olive oil
4 lamb shanks, 2kg (4½lb) in total
Sea salt
pinch of saffron
2 onions, peeled and chopped
3 fat cloves garlic, peeled and sliced
570ml (1 pint) full-bodied fruity red Fairtrade wine
2 tbsp Fairtrade honey

2 Fairtrade cinnamon sticks
¼ tsp crushed dried chilli flakes
2 fresh bay leaves
800g (1 ¾lb) chopped tinned tomatoes in natural juice
410g (14¼oz) tin chickpeas in water, drained
small bunch fresh flat-leaf parsley, stalks discarded
2 preserved lemons, chopped

## METHOD

**Preheat** the oven to 180°C/350°F/Gas Mark 4. Heat 2 tbsp of the oil in a large lidded flameproof casserole with a capacity of at least 3.5 litres (6 pints) until sizzling.

**Season** the lamb with a sprinkling of sea salt. Brown two of the shanks on all sides for about 10 minutes, then transfer them to a plate. Repeat with the other two shanks, and then discard the fat from the casserole. Put the saffron in a cup and leave to soak in 1 tbsp of the red wine.

**Wipe** the casserole and add 2 tbsp oil. Add the onion and garlic and cook until soft. Add the saffron (and soaking liquid), honey, cinnamon, chilli, bay leaves, and the rest of the wine. Simmer for 2–3 minutes. Stir in the tomatoes. Submerge the lamb shanks in the liquid. Bring back to the boil, cover, and place in the oven for 45 minutes. Turn the lamb, stir in the chickpeas, and reduce the oven temperature to 150°C/300°F/Gas Mark 2. Cook for another 1–1½ hours or until the lamb is tender.

**Stir** the parsley and preserved lemons into the sauce, taste to check the seasoning, and serve.

# GREEN BANANA CURRY

## INGREDIENTS

Serves 4
Preparation time 5 minutes
Cooking time 30 minutes

5 green (underripe) Fairtrade bananas, peeled
2–3 tbsp vegetable oil

1 onion, finely sliced
1 tbsp curry paste, such as Tikka
400 ml (14fl oz) can coconut milk
Salt and freshly ground Fairtrade black pepper
3 tbsp chopped fresh coriander to garnish

## METHOD

**Slice** the banana into 2.5cm (1in) slices.

**Heat** the oil in a deep frying pan and fry the banana slices, in batches, until lightly browned on each side.

**Set** the fried bananas aside on a plate lined with kitchen paper.

**Add** the onion to the pan and cook it for 10 minutes until soft, stirring occasionally.

**Return** the banana slices to the pan and stir in the curry paste.

**Add** half the coconut milk and stir well. Cook for 10 minutes over a low heat, then add the seasoning.

**Pour** in the remaining coconut milk and let the mixture simmer until it thickens and the bananas break down a little.

**Garnish** with coriander and serve immediately with cooked Fairtrade basmati rice.

*Tip* You could also garnish this with wedges of Fairtrade lime.

**Judges' note** This is gorgeous.

## SO SIMPLE, AND ONLY A HANDFUL OF INGREDIENTS

**Vanessa Hewitt** from Manley, Cheshire

# CUBAN ORANGE CHICKEN

## INGREDIENTS

Serves 6–8
Preparation time 10 minutes
(plus 2 hours marinating time)
Cooking time 1 hour

2 tsp salt
1 tsp Fairtrade black pepper

½ tsp garlic salt
1–1.5kg (2¼lb–3lb 3oz) chicken, cut into serving pieces
240ml (8fl oz) juice from Fairtrade oranges
Juice of one Fairtrade lime

## METHOD

**Measure** salt, pepper, and garlic salt into a small bowl and combine.

**Arrange** the chicken in a deep wide dish and sprinkle both sides of the pieces with the salt mixture. Set aside.

**Pour** the combined juices over the chicken and leave it to marinate, covered, in the refrigerator. After one hour turn the pieces and leave them to marinate for another hour.

**Preheat** the oven to 190°C/375°F/Gas Mark 5 near the end of the marinating time. Remove the chicken from the dish and arrange it in a baking pan.

**Pour** the marinade juice off into a measuring jug. Drizzle half of the juice over the chicken, and place it in the oven.

**Baste** the chicken after 30 minutes with the remaining juice and roast for a further 30 minutes.

# SPICED POTATO PATTIES

## INGREDIENTS

Makes 16 patties
Preparation time 15 minutes
Cooking time 20 minutes

4 potatoes, 600g (1lb 5oz) total, peeled
   and cut into cubes
4 tbsp olive oil
1 onion, finely chopped
1 tsp mustard seeds
6 fresh curry leaves, or freeze-dried curry
   leaves (Karavepelei leaves)

1 tbsp curry powder
½ tsp Fairtrade turmeric (haldi powder)
1 leek, shredded
salt and freshly ground Fairtrade black
   pepper
250g (9oz) plain flour
Vegetable oil for deep frying
Fairtrade mango chutney, to serve

## METHOD

**Steam** the potatoes for 10–15 minutes until cooked through.

**Heat** half the oil in a large frying pan meanwhile and add the onion, mustard seeds, and curry leaves. Cook for a minute or so until the mustard seeds start to pop.

**Add** the curry powder and turmeric to the onion. Stir well, and then add the leek and fry until the vegetables are just tender.

**Add** the potatoes to the frying pan when they are cooked, along with plenty of seasoning. Mix well then divide into 16 portions and set aside.

**Measure** the flour into a bowl and gradually stir in the remaining oil and 125ml (4½fl oz) water, stirring all the while. Then gather it together (this is easier with your hands) to form a firm dough.

**Pour** enough vegetable oil into a large pan to fill it one-third full and put it over a medium heat.

**Divide** the dough into 16 balls. On a lightly floured surface roll each ball out to a 12cm (5in) circle. Top with one of the potato portions. Fold over the pastry to give you a semi-circle, press the edges down, and crimp with a fork. Repeat with the remaining pastry and filling.

**When** the oil is hot, deep-fry the patties carefully in batches for 3 minutes until golden brown. Drain on kitchen paper, and allow to cool before serving.

*Tip* These patties would also make a quick, easy, and tasty supper. If you like, you could serve them with Fairtrade mango chutney.

**Mrs Meenadchianmah Selvathurai** from Liverpool

# RICHARD'S SWEET AND SOUR PORK RIBS

## Sheherazade Goldsmith

I rear and grow most produce at the farm myself, but there are some key elements that can only come from abroad. Most are grown by Fairtrade co-operatives. Choosing Fairtrade produce gives us the opportunity to repay those who provide us with unique, exotic ingredients we would otherwise have to do without. For me there is no other choice.

## INGREDIENTS

Serves 4
Preparation time 20 minutes
Cooking time 1 hour

1 tbsp groundnut oil
1 red onion, finely sliced
7.5cm (3in) piece root ginger, peeled and chopped very finely
1 small red chilli, chopped very finely
3 garlic cloves, finely sliced

pinch of Chinese five-spice powder
½ tsp Sichuan pepper, ground using a pestle and mortar
1 tbsp white wine vinegar
2 tbsp Fairtrade honey
1 tsp tomato purée
2 tsp soy sauce
500g–1kg (1lb 2oz–2¼lb) organic pork ribs, divided into single rib pieces

## METHOD

**Preheat** oven to 170°C/340°F/Gas Mark 3. Pour the groundnut oil into a saucepan over a medium heat. Add the onion and cook until soft. Add the ginger, chilli, and garlic, and cook for 2 minutes. Then add the Chinese five-spice powder and ground Sichuan pepper.

**Add** the white wine vinegar. Let the mixture come to the boil, and then add the honey, tomato purée, and soy sauce. Leave it to cook for a while to allow the flavours to infuse. Then taste it, and adjust it to your liking. (See tip.)

**Arrange** the pork rib pieces in a roasting tray, and pour three-quarters of the sauce over them.

**Place** in the oven for at least one hour. Check every 15 minutes, giving them a stir and, if necessary, adding a little water to prevent them drying out. They are ready to eat when the ribs are glazed with the sticky sauce.

**Heat** the remaining sauce and pour it over the ribs just before serving.

*Tip* You could marinate the ribs in the sauce, for as little as 20 minutes if you like, before you roast them.

# QUINOA WITH MOROCCAN SAUCE

## INGREDIENTS

Serves 3-4
Preparation time 15 minutes
Cooking time 25 minutes

1 tsp each Fairtrade ground cinnamon,
    Fairtrade ground ginger, Fairtrade
    ground turmeric, freshly ground
    Fairtrade nutmeg, freshly ground
    Fairtrade black pepper, ground cumin,
    ground coriander, paprika, and caraway
    seeds
generous pinch each ground cloves and
    saffron strands
3 cloves garlic, finely chopped
1 small chilli, finely chopped

2 tbsp olive oil
400g (13½oz) tin chopped tomatoes
410g (14½oz) tin chickpeas, drained
150ml (5fl oz) vegetable stock
100g (3½oz) Fairtrade organic dates,
    coarsely chopped
250g (9oz) Fairtrade quinoa
1 tbsp Fairtrade honey
1 handful fresh coriander, roughly
    chopped
450g (1lb) steamed or roasted
    vegetables, such as butternut squash,
    carrots, parsnips, or courgettes, cut
    into bite-sized chunks

## METHOD

**Mix** together all the spices with the garlic and chilli in a bowl, and set aside.

**Heat** the oil in a large saucepan and add the spice mixture. Cook for 3–5 minutes, over a gentle heat, stirring constantly.

**Add** the tomatoes, chickpeas, stock, and dates. Bring up to the boil, reduce the heat, and simmer for 20 minutes. If after this time the sauce is too thick add a splash of water. Meanwhile cook the quinoa according to the pack instructions.

**Stir** the honey into the tomato sauce, and sprinkle with the coriander.

**Stir** the cooked vegetables into the sauce, allow them to heat through, and serve with the quinoa.

*Tip* You can deseed the chilli if you do not like your food to be too hot.

**Judges' note** This is a great recipe for using up left-over cooked vegetables.

**S Gilbey** from Bridport, Dorset

# CHICKEN MOLE

## INGREDIENTS

Serves 4
Preparation time 15 minutes
Cooking time 1 hour

2 tbsp olive oil
5 garlic cloves, crushed
3 medium onions, roughly chopped
1 tsp each Fairtrade ground cinnamon,
  ground coriander, ground cumin, and
  Fairtrade dried oregano
½tsp of each ground cloves and salt
1 star anise

6 red chillies, deseeded and finely
  chopped
75g (2½oz) flaked almonds
50g (1¾oz) Fairtrade raisins
50g (1¾ oz) Fairtrade dark chocolate,
  chopped
400g (14oz) tin chopped tomatoes
8 bone-in chicken thighs, or 4 chicken
  portions
15g (½oz) fresh flat-leaf parsley or
  coriander, roughly chopped

## METHOD

**Preheat** the oven to 180°C/350°F/Gas Mark 4.

**Heat** 1 tbsp of the oil. Add the garlic and half the onion and cook gently for 8–10 minutes until soft.

**Add** all the spices, salt, star anise, and chillies. Cook for 2–3 minutes until fragrant. Then add the almonds, raisins, chocolate, and tomatoes along with 200ml (7fl oz) of water.

**Bring** to the boil and simmer for 15 minutes.

**Heat** the other tbsp of oil in another frying pan. Add the rest of the onions and the chicken. Cook, turning and stirring, until they are browned.

**Place** the chicken and onions in a medium roasting tin.

**Pour** the sauce ingredients into a food processor, or use a hand blender, and purée until smooth. Cover the chicken in sauce and bake in the oven for 30 minutes.

**Sprinkle** with the chopped parsley or coriander to serve.

*Tip* This is a simplified but authentic version of the Mexican classic, and it goes well with a salad.

**Judges' note** Although this recipe isn't a visual feast it tastes terrific.

**Elena Greenwood** from Stratford-upon-Avon

# NORTH AFRICAN CHICKEN WITH CRISPED PEPPERS AND GREENS

## INGREDIENTS

Serves 4
Preparation time 15 minutes
Cooking time 25 minutes

½ tsp each ground allspice, coriander, and cumin
1 tsp paprika
Salt and freshly ground Fairtrade black pepper
1 large clove garlic, finely chopped
450–700g (1–1½lb) boneless, skinless chicken breast, cut crosswise into 1.5cm (¾in) strips

4 tbsp extra virgin olive oil
2 large red Fairtrade peppers, deseeded and thinly sliced
2–3 red chillies, deseeded and thinly sliced
2 very big handfuls (about 140g/5oz) spring greens
1 small to medium onion, thinly sliced

## METHOD

**Slip** one large 30 x 45cm (12 x 18in) roasting tin, or two smaller shallow baking dishes into the oven to heat, and turn the oven on to 220°C/475°F/Gas Mark 7.

**Toss** together the spices in a large bowl with a generous amount of black pepper, the garlic, chicken, and olive oil.

**Stir** in the peppers, spring greens, and sliced onion, and toss to blend.

**Spread** the ingredients on the tin or dishes, taking care not to burn yourself. Make sure the pieces are spaced apart to help the crisping process.

**Roast** in the oven for 20–25 minutes, turning occasionally until the chicken is cooked. The greens should be crisp.

**Serve** with cooked brown rice.

*Tip* This lovely colourful dish would go wonderfully with Fairtrade brown rice.

**Judges' note** Make sure you use a large enough roasting tin so the ingredients have plenty of room to roast, and not poach. A delicious dish.

**Shirley Hodge** from Glasgow

# FILLET OF BEEF WITH CHAMP AND A HONEY AND STOUT GRAVY

## Noel McMeel

This is a great dish to prepare, not just for a family Sunday dinner but so easy to prepare in advance. This can be served with your own favourite vegetables.

## INGREDIENTS

Serves 4
Preparation time 20 minutes
Cooking time 35 minutes

**Champ**
4 large floury potatoes, peeled and washed
100ml (3½fl oz) whipping cre am
4 spring onions, chopped
50g (1¾oz) salted butter

**Beef**
4 fillet steaks, 200g (7oz) each
A little rapeseed oil
Salt and Fairtrade black pepper

**Gravy**
330ml (11fl oz) Irish stout
4 tbsp Fairtrade honey
Sprig each of rosemary and thyme
2 garlic cloves, roughly chopped

## METHOD

**Make** the champ. Cook the potatoes in a saucepan of boiling salted water for about 20 minutes until soft, then drain and mash them until smooth. Bring the cream and spring onions to the boil in a saucepan, add to the mash, and beat until smooth. Add the butter, season, and keep warm.

**Preheat** the oven to 200°C/400°F/Gas Mark 6 and heat a baking tray. Season the steaks on both sides. Heat a heavy frying pan until very hot, and add a little oil. Place the steaks in the pan and sear all over (top, bottom, and sides), then transfer to the hot baking tray and finish cooking in the oven. Allow 4–5 minutes for medium-rare meat.

**Make** the gravy. Deglaze the steak juices in the frying pan with the stout and then boil to reduce by about three-quarters. Add the honey, rosemary, thyme and garlic, and then simmer for 5 minutes. Strain and season, then keep hot. Remove the steaks from the oven and leave to rest for a few minutes.

**Serve** the steaks with a scoop of champ and the honey and stout gravy.

# MUSHROOM STROGANOFF

## INGREDIENTS

Serves 3–4
Preparation time 15 minutes
Cooking time 20–25 minutes

250g (9oz) Fairtrade long-grain rice
2 medium onions, chopped
2 cloves garlic, crushed
4 Fairtrade cardamom pods, bruised

500g (1lb 2oz) mushrooms, sliced
2 tbsp vegetable oil
1 tsp chilli oil (optional – but does add a
  zing to the dish)
20g (¾oz) cornflour
300ml (10fl oz) carton double cream
Salt and Fairtrade pepper

## METHOD

**Cook** the rice according to the packet instructions. Meanwhile, fry the onions, garlic, and cardamom pods in the vegetable and chilli oils in a large deep-sided frying pan over a medium heat for about 8 minutes, until soft but not browned.

**Add** the mushrooms and continue to cook for about 7–8 minutes until they are soft.

**Remove** the pan from the heat and allow to cool slightly.

**Place** the cornflour in a bowl and enough water to make a paste. Add the paste slowly to the cooled mushroom mixture, stirring all the time.

**Add** the double cream and simmer gently until thickened, adding a splash of water if needed.

**Season** to taste before serving with the cooked rice.

*Tip* Finish this dish with a generous sprinkling of chopped flat-leaf parsley and a squeeze or two of Fairtrade lemon juice.

**Pauline Chambers** from Driffield, East Yorkshire

# LAMB TAGINE

## Joanne Harris

I'm an enthusiastic supporter of the work of the Fairtrade Foundation as it's all about underlining the connection between what we eat and the people who produce it, who are often exploited. When you buy a product with the FAIRTRADE Mark, it means the producer has received a fair price for it. By buying Fairtrade, you're helping lift whole communities out of poverty, improving the lives of seven million people around the globe. It's so important for people to know that coffee doesn't grow in packets and pineapples don't grow in supermarkets. In Britain, we do seem to lack an awareness of the origins of our food and it is high time we started to pay attention to what we eat, where it comes from, and the lives of the people that bring it to us.

## INGREDIENTS

Serves 6
Preparation time 10 minutes
Cooking time approximately 1 hour
20 minutes

2 tbsp olive oil
1 onion, chopped
600g (1lb 5oz) lamb, diced
½ tsp ground coriander

1 Fairtrade cinnamon stick
½ tsp Fairtrade ground ginger
6 Fairtrade cloves
½ tsp Fairtrade ground turmeric
Salt and Fairtrade black pepper
12 Fairtrade dried apricots
2 tbsp Fairtrade honey

## METHOD

**Heat** the oil in a large pan with a lid and add the onion and lamb and cook until the lamb is browned all over. (You may want to cook the lamb in batches.)

**Add** the coriander, cinnamon stick, ginger, cloves, and turmeric and stir. Cook for another minute or two.

**Pour** in enough water to cover the lamb, add the salt and pepper, and bring to a simmer.

**Cover** and simmer for around 90 minutes. Then add the apricots and simmer for a further 30 minutes. Add more water if it becomes too dry.

**Remove** the cover and add the honey. Simmer for a further 10 minutes to reduce the liquid. Serve with couscous or rice.

*Tip* You don't need to have all the spices to make this recipe. Any three from the five should suffice.

# BAKED PENNE WITH DOLCELATTE CHEESE AND RADICCHIO

## Sir Steve Redgrave

As an athlete, I have always thought it's so important to be aware of the origins of my food, which is why I look for the FAIRTRADE Mark when I go shopping. With the nature of my work I have been lucky enough to travel around the world and have experience of the communities that Fairtrade helps. It made me put into context the massive impact that something as small as my weekly shop can have.

## INGREDIENTS

Serves 4
Preparation time 15 minutes
Cooking time 12–15 minutes

50g (1¾oz) butter, plus extra for greasing
250g (9oz) dried *penne rigate*
250g (9oz) button mushrooms, sliced
1 Fairtrade red pepper, sliced
2 garlic cloves, finely chopped

1 tbsp finely chopped fresh sage
1 small head of radicchio, weighing 250–275g (9–10oz), cored and finely shredded
250ml (8fl oz) double cream
50g (1¾oz) Parmesan cheese, grated
175g (6oz) Dolcelatte cheese, cubed
Salt and freshly ground Fairtrade black pepper
Fresh sage leaves, to garnish

## METHOD

**Put** a large saucepan of water on to boil. Preheat the oven to 220°C/425°F/Gas Mark 7. Butter a 23 x 28cm (9 x 11in) ovenproof dish and set aside. When the water has come to a boil add the pasta and cook until it is just al dente, according to the instructions on the pack.

**Melt** the butter in a large frying pan meanwhile, and fry the mushrooms, pepper, and garlic for about five minutes until softened. Stir in the sage and radicchio and remove the pan from the heat.

**Combine** the cream, Parmesan, and Dolcelatte together in a very large bowl and set it aside. When the pasta has cooked drain it thoroughly.

**Add** the mushroom mixture and the cooked pasta to the cheese mixture and stir to combine. Taste and adjust the seasoning.

**Transfer** the mixture to the ovenproof dish and bake in the oven for 12–15 minutes, or until the top is browned and bubbly. Garnish with the fresh sage leaves to serve.

# THAI FISH CURRY

## INGREDIENTS

Serves 4
Preparation time 20 minutes
Cooking time 15 minutes

2 red chillies, finely chopped
1 Fairtrade lime, juice and zest
2 stems lemongrass, chopped roughly
1 piece root ginger about the size of a
    walnut, peeled and chopped roughly

4 cloves garlic, peeled
1 small onion, peeled and thinly sliced
1 tbsp Thai fish sauce (or more to taste)
400ml (14fl oz) tin coconut milk
900g (2lb) firm white fish – my favourite
    is No Catch Cod – in roughly 3cm
    (1in) cubes
1 large Fairtrade mango, peeled and cut
    into roughly 2cm (¾in) cubes

## METHOD

**Make** a curry paste first. Put the chillies, lime, lemongrass, ginger root, garlic, onion, and fish sauce into a blender. Whizz it all together until you get a smooth paste.

**Heat** a large frying pan or wok, add the paste and sizzle for a minute or so, stirring so it doesn't stick.

**Pour** in the coconut milk. Mix well and bring to a simmer.

**Add** the fish, trying not to break up the pieces, and simmer for around 5 minutes.

**Add** the mango and keep simmering for another couple of minutes. Add more fish sauce or lime juice, to taste.

**Sit** down, eat, and enjoy.

**Serve** with Fairtrade rice, ideally Himalayan basmati, or some other Thai fragrant rice.

*Tip* You can garnish this dish with some freshly chopped coriander. You could also substitute a Fairtrade pineapple for the mango, and use prawns instead of white fish.

**Karen Darnton** from Clevedon, Somerset

# SLOW-ROAST SHOULDER OF PORK WITH QUINCES OR APPLES

## Sophie Grigson

This recipe is an autumn favourite of mine, a superb one-pot dish that cooks to a gorgeous tenderness in the slow heat of the oven. It's best made with quinces, but if you can't get any, or if you wish to make the dish at other times of the year, replace them with eating apples or pears, adding them to the dish only after the first hour of cooking, and making sure they are completely coated in juices before returning the pan to the oven. More than that, nearly all the ingredients can be purchased from local producers or are Fairtrade classics, like cinnamon or sugar.

## INGREDIENTS

Serves 6
Preparation time 15 minutes
Cooking time 2 hours

1.25-1.5kg (2¾–3lb 3oz) boned shoulder of pork
550g (1¼lb) quinces (2 fairly large ones) or Fairtrade eating apples or pears (see Introduction, above)
2 red onions, halved and thickly sliced
2 medium chillies, seeded and cut into strips
4 fat cloves garlic, sliced
3 bay leaves
2 Fairtrade cinnamon sticks
2 tbsp olive oil
60g Fairtrade Demerara sugar
2 tbsp white wine vinegar
100ml (3½ fl oz) Fairtrade white wine
Salt and Fairtrade black pepper

## METHOD

**Preheat** the oven to 180°C/350°F/Gas Mark 4. If the shoulder has been rolled remove the string. Using a sharp knife make criss-cross slashes about 2-3 cm (¾-1in) apart in the skin. Grease a baking dish lightly. Lay the pork in it, skin upwards.

**Peel** the quinces then quarter and core. Cut each quarter into 2 or 3 slices depending on size. Tumble the quince slices, onion, chillies, garlic, bay leaves, and cinnamon sticks around the pork. Mix the oil, sugars, vinegar, wine, salt, and pepper and spoon over the pork and quinces and onions. Cover with silver foil and slide into the oven. Roast for 1 hour, remove the foil and baste both pork and quinces and onions with their own juices. Return to the oven, uncovered, for a further hour, basting occasionally.

**When** the pork is very tender, and the quinces are soft as butter turn off the oven. Prop the door ajar and leave to rest for 10-20 minutes before carving and serving.

# VEGETABLE AND CHICKEN PIE

## INGREDIENTS

Serves 2
Preparation time 10 minutes
Cooking time 45 minutes

**Filling**
40g (1½oz) butter
1 Fairtrade red pepper, thinly sliced
1 leek, sliced
¼tsp Fairtrade ground turmeric
40g (1½oz) plain flour
250ml (8fl oz) milk

200g (7oz) tub crème fraîche
150g (5½oz) green beans, cut into 2cm
  (¾in) pieces and blanched
225g (8oz) cooked chicken, sliced
  (or 2–3 chicken thigh fillets, cooked)
**Potato topping**
450g (1lb) large potatoes, peeled and cut
  into large chunks
A large knob of butter
4–5 tbsp milk
Salt and Fairtrade black pepper

## METHOD

**Preheat** the oven to 200°C/400°F/Gas Mark 6. Cook the potatoes in boiling salted water until tender. Then drain and mash them with the butter and enough milk to make a thick mash. Season with salt.

**Melt** the butter in a large pan. Add the pepper and leek, and cook for 3–4 minutes until soft.

**Stir** in the turmeric, cook for a minute, then add the flour and cook for a further 2–3 minutes.

**Pour** in the milk slowly while stirring constantly and cook for 4–5 minutes until thickened.

**Add** the crème fraîche, green beans, and cooked chicken, and mix well.

**Season** well and pour into a small ovenproof dish and cover with mashed potato.

**Place** in the oven and cook for 25 minutes until hot.

# GREAT FOR USING UP ODDS AND ENDS IN THE FRIDGE

**F McGee** from Stafford

# BEEF, MANGO, AND CELERY IN RED WINE

## Eileen Maybin

I chose this recipe because I love the combination of beef and wine, and like to have some in the freezer for when guests come to stay. There are now so many new Fairtrade ingredients, and they make this recipe taste better still. Although it takes a long time to cook it is quick to prepare. It also keeps extremely well overnight in the fridge, so it is a good dish when you want to get a course ready in advance.

## INGREDIENTS

Serves 4
Preparation time 45 minutes
Cooking time 1 hour

800g (1¾lb) beef, cut in chunks
4 tbsp flour, seasoned with salt and
   Fairtrade black pepper
5 tbsp olive oil
1 small onion, chopped
200g (7oz) mushrooms
500ml (16fl oz) Fairtrade red wine

150g (5½oz) bacon, diced
4 large stalks celery
100g (3½oz) Fairtrade dried mango
100g (3½oz) sun-dried tomatoes
2 tsp Fairtrade dried basil
2 tsp Fairtrade dried oregano
Several slices of zest from a Fairtrade
   orange, best discarded after cooking
500ml (16fl oz) stock

## METHOD

**Toss** the beef in seasoned flour, until the beef is evenly coated. Heat the oil until very hot in a heavy-bottomed saucepan. Brown the beef in three batches until well cooked all over. Remove from the pan and set aside.

**Add** the onion to the pan, and then the mushrooms. Cook until the onion is brown.

**Pour** the red wine into the saucepan, scraping the bottom for any remains of the fried meat. Add the bacon, celery, dried mango, sun-dried tomatoes, basil, oregano, and orange zest. Stir well, then add the stock. Reduce to a very low heat, cover and cook for one hour, or until the meat is tender. Stir occasionally to prevent the meat sticking to the bottom of the saucepan, and add water if necessary.

*Tip* You can serve this with Fairtrade basmati rice.

# CHEESY RICE BALLS IN TOMATO SAUCE

## INGREDIENTS

Serves 2-3
Preparation time 15 minutes
Cooking time 1 hour

170g (6oz) Fairtrade long-grain rice
1 small egg
1 tbsp plain flour
Salt and Fairtrade black pepper
200g (7oz) mozzarella, cut into
  small cubes

Sauce
25g (1oz) butter
1 medium onion, chopped
1 Fairtrade red pepper, diced
150ml (5fl oz) Fairtrade dry white wine
150ml (5fl oz) vegetable stock
400g (14oz) tin chopped tomatoes
  with herbs

## METHOD

**Boil** the rice until it is cooked, according to the packet instructions. Drain and set aside to cool.

**Preheat** the oven to 180°C/350°F/Gas Mark 4. Make the sauce first by heating the butter in a saucepan. Add the onion and red pepper, and fry for 5 minutes.

**Add** the wine and stock. Bring to the boil and keep boiling until reduced by half.

**Add** the tomatoes, season with black pepper if desired, and turn down the heat. Simmer, covered, for 20 minutes.

**Mix** the cooled rice with the egg and flour and season generously. Divide the mixture into six piles and then shape them into balls.

**Set** aside half of the mozzarella cubes. Divide the remaining cubes into six portions and push the cubes into each ball. Enclose any holes with the rice.

**Spoon** the tomato sauce into an ovenproof dish and top with the rice balls. Sprinkle with the remaining cheese. Cover and place in the oven and bake for 25 minutes.

*Tip* You could add a sprinkling of Parmesan before baking and finish with a few fresh basil leaves.

**Kim Nash** from Portslade, Brighton

# FAIR-LY FRUITY COCONUT CURRY

## INGREDIENTS

Serves 3-4
Preparation time 20 minutes
Cooking time 30 minutes

250g (9oz) Fairtrade Thai jasmine rice, boiled or steamed
1 tbsp sunflower oil
2 cloves garlic, crushed
2 tbsp Thai red curry paste
450g (1lb) raw king prawns, shelled (defrosted if frozen)

Half a Fairtrade pineapple, peeled, cored, and cut into 2cm (¾in) cubes
400ml (14fl oz) can coconut milk, shaken before opening
1 large, firm Fairtrade banana, peeled and cut into thick diagonal slices
1 firm Fairtrade mango, peeled, stone removed, cut into 2cm (¾in) cubes

**To serve**
1 Fairtrade lime, cut into wedges

## METHOD

**Cook** the rice according to the packet instructions. Meanwhile heat a wok until it just smokes, then add the oil.

**Fry** the garlic for a few seconds over a medium heat. Add the red curry paste and stir-fry for another minute.

**Add** the prawns to the wok and stir-fry for 3 minutes before adding the pineapple cubes.

**Pour** in the coconut milk. Bring up to the boil and simmer for 5 minutes, stirring constantly.

**Add** the banana and mango and heat through for 2 minutes, continuing to stir.

**Serve** straight away on the bed of rice, with wedges of lime on the side.

**Katie J Down** from Cambridge

# FRUITY NORTH AFRICAN SALAD

## INGREDIENTS

Serves 4 as a main course,
6-8 as a starter
Preparation time 20 minutes
Cooking time 20 minutes plus 30
minutes standing time

175g (6oz) Fairtrade brown basmati rice
I Fairtrade orange, juice only
1 tbsp Fairtrade honey

410g (14¼oz) tin chickpeas, drained
50g (1¾oz) dried cranberries
50g (1¾oz) Fairtrade sultanas
50g (1¾oz) Fairtrade dates, chopped
2 large tomatoes, skinned and roughly
   chopped
1 Fairtrade green pepper, finely chopped
3-4 tbsp roughly chopped fresh
   coriander

## METHOD

Cook the rice according to packet instructions, drain, and place in a large bowl.

Whisk the orange juice and honey together, and pour over the warm rice. Set aside to cool.

Add all the remaining ingredients to the bowl after a few minutes and mix well.

Allow the salad to stand for half an hour so that the dried fruit has a chance to plump up.

*Tip* This could be served in toasted pitta breads with a spoonful of yoghurt.

Judges' note A great recipe for children – ideal for packed lunches too.

# COLOURFUL, FRUITY, NUTRITIOUS, AND FAIR

**Anna Heywood** from Hay on Wye, Powys

# ROAST LEMON-HERB CHICKEN IN WINE

## INGREDIENTS

Serves 4
Preparation time 15 minutes
Cooking time 1 hour 40 minutes

1 chicken, weighing approximately 1kg
(2¼lb)
30g (1oz) butter, softened
1 clove garlic, crushed
3 tbsp Fairtrade dried oregano

Juice of 1 Fairtrade lemon
Juice of 1 Fairtrade lime
Fairtrade black pepper, freshly ground

**Herb Wine Sauce**
30g (1oz) butter
1 small onion, finely chopped
500ml (16fl oz) Fairtrade white wine
250ml (8fl oz) hot chicken stock

## METHOD

**Preheat** the oven to 200°C/400°F/Gas Mark 6. Place the chicken in a large roasting dish.

**Mix** the butter, garlic, and 2 tbsp of the oregano in a small bowl to make a paste. Then stir in the juice of the lemon and the lime.

**Gently** ease the skin away from the breasts at the neck cavity and smear half the paste onto the breasts under the skin. Smear the remaining paste all over the chicken.

**Place** the squeezed lemon and limes into the cavity of the chicken.

**Make** the Herb Wine Sauce now by heating the butter in a frying pan. Add the onion and gently cook until soft. Stir in half of the wine and all of the stock. Pour the sauce directly into the roasting dish all around the chicken. Season the chicken well with a good grinding of Fairtrade black pepper and sprinkle the remaining oregano all over the chicken.

**Cover** the chicken with foil, and place it in the oven. After 45 minutes, remove the chicken from the oven and stir the rest of the wine into the cooking juices.

**Reduce** the temperature to 150°C/300°F/Gas Mark 2, and cook the chicken for another 45 minutes. Then remove the foil and cook for a final 10 minutes. Remove from the oven and allow to rest for 10 minutes before carving. Pour the remaining sauce from the roasting dish into a gravy jug, spooning off any fat.

**Serve** the chicken with Fairtrade basmati rice and seasonal greens.

*Tip* If you like, you can add the zest from the lemon and the lime to the butter paste. To test whether chicken is cooked, pierce the thickest part with a knife. The juices will run clear if the chicken is cooked.

**Markus Schneider** from London

# FRAGRANT RICE

## George Alagiah

"Let's go for a curry!" They are the words that so often precede an evening out. The emphasis is on the curry. In my family, when we were growing up in Sri Lanka, we always talked about having "rice and curry". The two things went always together, as inseparable as "sausage and mash". As long as you're cooking Fairtrade basmati you're doing more than pandering to your taste buds. I've been Patron of the Fairtrade Foundation for years now and it's one of the most creative things I do. Fairtrade is about putting right some of the poverty I witnessed as a foreign correspondent.

## INGREDIENTS

Serves 4
Preparation time 10 minutes
Cooking time 30 minutes

250g (9oz) Fairtrade basmati rice
Knob of butter
1 medium onion, finely chopped

2 Fairtrade cinnamon sticks
4 Fairtrade cloves
1 Fairtrade lemon, zest only
Handful Fairtrade raisins or finely
   chopped Fairtrade dried apricots
Pinch of salt

## METHOD

**Rinse** the rice under running water and set aside.

**Melt** the butter in a saucepan over a low heat and add the onion. Fry gently for 5 minutes.

**Add** the rice and all the other ingredients and fry for 2–3 minutes.

**Add** 500ml (16fl oz) of water and the salt, and bring to the boil.

**Reduce** to a very low simmer and cook for around 18 minutes.

**Drain** and serve.

*Tip* In this recipe, the rice is a dish in its own right, but it can be used as an accompaniment for a chicken or fish.

# ORANGE-COATED CHICKEN WITH MANGO SALSA

## INGREDIENTS

Serves 4
Preparation time 20–25 minutes
Cooking time 15 minutes

### Mango salsa

1 large Fairtrade mango, peeled, stone removed, and diced
2 large red chillies, deseeded and finely chopped
4 spring onions, chopped

2 tsp Fairtrade brown sugar
2 Fairtrade oranges, juice and zest
8 tbsp olive oil

### Orange-coated chicken

4 chicken breasts, skinless and boneless
3 tbsp plain flour
2 medium eggs, beaten
150g (5½oz) breadcrumbs

## METHOD

**Mix** the mango in a small bowl with the chillies, spring onions, sugar, 2 tbsp of the orange juice and 2 tbsp of the olive oil. Cover with cling film and chill in the refrigerator until needed.

**Flatten** the chicken breasts by lightly bashing them with a rolling pin between cling film. Place the flour in one bowl, and whisk the egg and remaining orange juice together in another. Mix the breadcrumbs and orange zest in a third bowl.

**Coat** each piece in flour, then egg, and finally in breadcrumbs, and set aside.

**Heat** the remaining oil in a large frying pan and cook the chicken for 10–12 minutes, turning halfway, until golden and thoroughly cooked.

**Serve** the chicken hot with the chilled mango salsa and a salad.

**Yvonne Findlay** from King's Lynn, Norfolk

# VEGETABLE BIRYANI

## INGREDIENTS

Serves 4
Preparation time 15 minutes
Cooking time about 30 minutes

### Spice paste
1 tsp each garam masala, cumin seeds, chilli powder, salt, Fairtrade ground black pepper, Fairtrade ground cinnamon, and ground coriander
3 tsp finely chopped garlic
Half a small onion, roughly chopped
2 tsp finely chopped fresh root ginger

### Biryani
4–5 sprays of cooking oil spray
1 small onion, finely chopped
4 Fairtrade cloves
2 Fairtrade cardamom pods
250g (9oz) frozen mixed vegetables
4 tomatoes, roughly chopped
250g (9oz) Fairtrade basmati rice, rinsed
3 tbsp flaked almonds, toasted
3 tbsp chopped fresh coriander

## METHOD

**Make** the spice paste first. Combine the garam masala, cumin seeds, chilli powder, salt, peppercorns, cinnamon, and coriander in a clean dry frying pan. Dry fry over a medium heat, stirring constantly, for 2–3 minutes or until well toasted without burning. Remove from the heat. Put the garlic, onion, ginger, and toasted spices into a blender with 2–3 tbsp water and blend to a fine paste and set aside.

**Spray** the base of a large saucepan with the cooking oil. Add the onions and cook, stirring, over a medium heat for 8 minutes until the onion has softened.

**Add** the spice paste along with the cloves and cardamom pods and cook, stirring all the time, for 5 minutes. Add the mixed vegetables and the tomatoes and cook for 5 minutes.

**Stir** in the rice. Pour over enough boiling water to cover. Bring to the boil, reduce the heat, cover, and simmer for 10–12 minutes, or until the rice is cooked.

**Sprinkle** over the almonds and the coriander and serve immediately.

**Ayse Babur-Puplett** from Newton Community Resource Centre, Stockton-on-Tees

# CHAPTER TWO

I MUST HAVE
SOMETHING
SWEET
RIGHT NOW!

# MICROWAVE CHOCCY BIKKIES

## INGREDIENTS

Makes 12–16
Preparation time 20 minutes
Cooking time 4½–5 minutes in an
850 watt microwave oven

100g (3½oz) butter
2 large eggs
200g (7oz) Fairtrade sugar

100g (3½oz) self-raising flour
35g (1¼oz) Fairtrade cocoa
50g (1¾oz) Fairtrade brazil nuts,
   almonds, or walnuts, chopped
2–3 drops Fairtrade vanilla extract or
   good-quality almond essence

## METHOD

**Melt** butter in microwave in a medium bowl.

**Add** the eggs and mix well. Then mix in the sugar followed by the flour.

**Stir** in the cocoa and mix well.

**Add** the nuts and the vanilla extract or almond essence and combine. Set aside.

**Line** a shallow 22cm (8¾in) ceramic microwaveable dish with all-purpose cling film. Add the mixture and cover it lightly with more cling film.

**Microwave** on full power for 4½–5 minutes.

**Remove** the cling film covering and leave to cool. Once the Bikkies are cold invert them onto a board, removing the remaining cling film.

**Dust** with icing sugar, cut into slices, and enjoy.

**Judges' note** These are deliciously squidgy – a cross between a brownie and a sponge.

# CONQUERS A CHOCOLATE CRAVING IN MINUTES

**Rosemary Kirk** from Newton Abbey

# CHOCOLATE CHIP BROWNIES

## INGREDIENTS

Makes 24 pieces
Preparation time 30 minutes
Cooking time 20–25 minutes

125g (4½oz) butter or margarine
200g (7oz) Fairtrade milk chocolate
200g (7oz) Fairtrade granulated sugar
120g (4oz) plain flour

30g (1oz) self-raising flour
2 large eggs, beaten
40g (1½oz) extra Fairtrade milk chocolate, chopped
40g (1½oz) Fairtrade white chocolate, chopped
1 tbsp Fairtrade cocoa

## METHOD

**Preheat** the oven to 180°C/350°F/Gas Mark 4.

**Grease** 23cm (9in) square cake tin and set it aside.

**Melt** the butter or margarine and 200g (7oz) milk chocolate together in a pan. Let it cool until it is just warm, and then stir in the sugar.

**Sift** the flours together in a mixing bowl and add the melted chocolate mixture.

**Stir** in the eggs and the chopped milk chocolate, and spread the mixture in the prepared tin.

**Sprinkle** the chopped white chocolate into the mixture and swirl it through with a teaspoon.

**Place** the tin in the oven and bake for 20–25 minutes.

**Cool** the brownies in the pan and then cut into 24 pieces.

**Dust** the brownies with cocoa powder.

**Danika Stow-Monk** from Southampton

# FRUITY JELLY

## INGREDIENTS

Serves 5
Preparation time 7 minutes
Cooking time 5 minutes plus setting
time

2 medium Fairtrade bananas, peeled and
sliced
1 medium Fairtrade mango, peeled,
stone removed, and diced

1 medium Fairtrade pineapple, peeled
and diced
500ml (16fl oz) Fairtrade Fruit Passion
Pure Tropical Juice
2 rounded tbsp agar flakes (from health
food shops)
1 tbsp Fairtrade clear honey or Fairtrade
white sugar (optional)

## METHOD

**Wet** the insides of five 100ml (3½fl oz) ramekins or moulds with water to ensure the jelly will come out cleanly.

**Divide** the bananas, mango, and pineapple between the prepared moulds. Set aside.

**Pour** the juice into a pan and sprinkle over the agar flakes. Bring to a simmer on a medium heat, but without stirring, until it reaches a simmer.

**Simmer** for 3–5 minutes, stirring occasionally, until the flakes dissolve.

**Add** the honey, or sugar if using, and stir until dissolved.

**Pour** into the prepared moulds and leave to set.

**Turn** onto a serving dish, garnishing with any leftover fruit.

*Tip* For a variation, you could use Fairtrade apple juice with diced mango, or try Fairtrade orange juice with chunky pineapple bits. If you are combining banana with apple juice, it's best to first dip the bananas in lemon juice (Fairtrade, of course) to prevent discoloration. This recipe provides a great way to help kids towards their five-a-day.

**Linda Hunter** from Darlington

# ORANGE AND CHOCOLATE PUDDING

## INGREDIENTS

Serves 6
Preparation time 20 minutes
Cooking time 10 minutes in 850 watt
microwave or 2 hours steaming

3 tbsp Fairtrade honey
2 large Fairtrade oranges, rind grated,
  peeled, and fruit sliced
175g (6oz) self-raising flour
100g (3½oz) Fairtrade granulated sugar

100g (3½oz) soft butter or margarine,
  plus extra for greasing
2 large eggs, beaten
100g (3½oz) Fairtrade chocolate, broken
  into small pieces

### Sauce
4 tbsp Fairtrade orange juice
2 tbsp cornflour
2 tbsp Fairtrade honey

## METHOD

**Grease** a 1.5litre (2¾pint) microwaveable basin and put the 3 tbsp honey into the base.

**Arrange** the slices of orange along the bottom and sides of the basin and set it aside.

**Beat** the flour, sugar, butter or margarine, eggs, and orange rind in a large bowl until creamy.

**Fold** in the chocolate and a little Fairtrade orange juice, if desired, and pour into the basin.

**Cover** with a lid and microwave at 850 watts for 10 minutes. Or, steam for two hours on the stove.

**For** the sauce, whisk the juice into the cornflour in a measuring jug, then make up to 275ml (9fl oz) with water. Add the 2 tbsp honey.

**Bring** the sauce to the boil in a pan, then simmer, stirring until the mixture turns syrupy. Serve the pudding drizzled with the sauce.

*Tip* To steam the pudding, place on a trivet in a large saucepan. Half fill with boiling water, cover tightly with a lid, and simmer for 2 hours. Check regularly and top up with water from the kettle as necessary.

**Brian Bury** from Rawtenstall, Lancashire

# ROSE AND VANILLA ICE CREAM

## INGREDIENTS

Serves 4
Preparation time 30 minutes
Cooking time 5–7 minutes plus
overnight freezing

100g (3½oz) caster sugar
2 egg yolks
15g (½oz) cornflour

600ml (1 generous pint) whole milk
Handful of Fairtrade rose petals, plus a
few extra to sprinkle at the end
A few drops of Fairtrade vanilla extract
150ml (5fl oz) double cream, lightly
whipped

## METHOD

**Whisk** the sugar with the egg yolks in a large bowl until they are pale and thick.

**Blend** the cornflour with a little milk until you have a smooth paste. Stir it into the egg mixture and set it aside.

**Place** the remaining milk in a saucepan with the rose petals and heat until just below boiling. Remove from the heat and let it cool a little. Then pour it slowly onto the egg mixture, stirring continuously. Return the mixture to the heat and bring to the boil. Then turn it down and simmer, stirring constantly until thickened (about 3 minutes). Remove from the heat.

**Pour** into a bowl and cover with cling film to prevent a skin forming. Leave to cool, then remove the cling film and strain the mixture to remove the rose petals.

**Stir** in the vanilla extract. Then pour into a freezer-proof container and freeze until ice crystals form and the mixture is slushy.

**Transfer** to a bowl and whisk or beat with a wooden spoon, then fold in the lightly whipped cream until it is evenly mixed in.

**Pour** into an ice cream container and freeze overnight.

**Allow** the ice cream to stand at room temperature for 10–15 minutes before serving to thaw and soften slightly. Sprinkle with a few extra petals.

*Tip* You can obtain organic dried rose petals from Steenbergs Organic. See page 219 for details.

**Sarah Hawtree, Emily Nicholls, and Rebecca Ward**
from Archbishop Holgate School, York

# APRICOT AND CHERRY LOAF

## INGREDIENTS

Makes one 900g (2lb) loaf
Preparation time 25 minutes
Cooking time 1 hour

175g (6oz) soft butter or margarine, plus extra for greasing

175g (6oz) caster sugar

Grated rind of an unwaxed Fairtrade lemon

3 medium eggs, beaten

175g (6oz) white self-raising flour

75g (2½oz) wholemeal self-raising flour

2 tbsp milk

8 glacé cherries, soaked to remove coating

40g (1½oz) mixed peel, soaked to remove coating

100g (3½oz) Fairtrade no-soak dried apricots, chopped

## METHOD

**Preheat** the oven to 180°C/350°F/Gas Mark 4. Grease and line a 900g (2lb) loaf tin.

**Beat** the butter or margarine and sugar to a pale and smooth mixture and add the lemon rind.

**Add** the beaten eggs to the mixture a little at a time.

**Sift** the flours and stir or fold them into the mixture.

**Add** enough milk to make a batter with a soft dropping consistency.

**Pat** dry the cherries and chop them into pieces the same size as the peel.

**Pat** dry the peel, then mix the cherries, peel, and apricots into the loaf batter.

**Spoon** the mixture into the prepared tin and level the top.

**Bake** for approximately 1 hour or until a skewer pushed into the middle comes out clean.

**Cool** for 15 minutes in the tin, then turn out onto a wire rack to finish cooling.

**Judges' note** If you are a cherry fan feel free to add more when you make the loaf.

**Sandra Lawrence** from Hayes, Middlesex

# SPICED BARS

## INGREDIENTS

Makes 16 bars
Preparation time 5 minutes
plus 2 hours setting
Cooking time 3-4 minutes

100g (3½oz) butter, diced
3 tbsp Fairtrade golden syrup (or
  Fairtrade honey)
1-2 tsp Fairtrade instant coffee

2 tsp Fairtrade ground cinnamon or
  mixed spice
200g (7oz) pack Rich Tea biscuits,
  crushed
50g (1¾oz) Fairtrade sultanas
50g (1¾oz) desiccated coconut
50g (1¾oz) icing sugar

## METHOD

**Grease** a 20 x 30cm (8 x 12in) baking tray or swiss roll tin with butter, and line it with a strip of greaseproof paper.

**Place** the butter and syrup (or honey) in a small pan with the coffee, cinnamon (or mixed spice), and 1 tbsp of water, and melt gently over a low heat until runny.

**Place** all the remaining ingredients in large bowl meanwhile and make a well in the centre.

**Pour** the melted butter mixture into the centre and combine.

**Press** the mixture into the prepared tin, allow to cool and chill for at least 2 hours until set.

# A GOOD RECIPE FOR ASPIRING YOUNG COOKS

**Bridget Mitchell** from Hindhead, Surrey

# A FAIR BANANA LOAF

## INGREDIENTS

Makes one 900g (2lb) loaf
Preparation time 20 minutes
Cooking time 1 hour

85g (3oz) butter
100g (3½oz) Fairtrade golden
   granulated sugar
2 large eggs, beaten

3 very ripe Fairtrade bananas, mashed
120ml (4fl oz) buttermilk
300g (10oz) self-raising flour
100g (3½oz) Fairtrade plain chocolate,
   roughly chopped
100g (3½oz) Fairtrade brazil nuts,
   roughly chopped
1 tsp Fairtrade vanilla extract

## METHOD

**Preheat** the oven to 180°C/350°F/Gas Mark 4. Grease a 900g (2lb) loaf tin and set aside.

**Cream** the butter and sugar. Beat the eggs in gradually.

**Stir** in the bananas and the buttermilk. Then gradually fold in the flour. Add in the chocolate, nuts, and vanilla extract and stir to combine.

**Tip** the mixture into the loaf tin and bake for 1 hour or until cooked – when a skewer inserted into the centre comes out clean.

**Leave** to cool slightly in the tin, then turn out onto a wire cooling rack.

**Serve** warm or cold.

**Judges' note** This would taste gorgeous spread with butter. It tastes even better after 2–3 days, as it allows the banana flavour time to develop.

# THIS IS A HONEY OF AN EVERYDAY, HOMELY TREAT

**Ms A Devine** from Leeds

# BANANA AND CHOCOLATE MUFFINS

## INGREDIENTS

Makes 12 large muffins
Preparation time 20 minutes
Cooking time 20-25 minutes

300g (10 oz) plain flour
1 tbsp baking powder
125g (4½oz) Fairtrade Demerara sugar

225ml (7½fl oz) milk
2 large eggs
125g (4½oz) butter, melted
2 Fairtrade bananas, mashed
100g (3½ oz) Fairtrade chocolate,
  chopped into small pieces

## METHOD

**Preheat** oven to 200°C/400°F/Gas 6. Place 12 muffin cases into a 12-hole muffin tin.

**Sieve** the flour into your mixing bowl.

**Add** the baking powder and stir. Add in the Demerara sugar, stir to combine, and set the bowl aside.

**Pour** the milk into a separate bowl or jug. Crack in the eggs and beat the mixture.

**Add** in the melted butter and stir. Add the mashed bananas and then the chopped chocolate and stir to combine.

**Add** the wet mixture to the dry mixture and stir well.

**Spoon** the batter into the 12 muffin cases, dividing it equally.

**Place** in the oven and bake for 20-25 minutes until well risen and golden.

**Enjoy!** (We did!)

**Beth and Gail Richards** from Bristol

# PEAR AND CHOCOLATE CAKE

## INGREDIENTS

Serves 6-8
Preparation time 30 minutes
Cooking time 50 minutes

125g (4½oz) soft butter or margarine
175g (6oz) golden caster sugar
4 large eggs, beaten
250g (9oz) self-raising wholemeal flour

50g (1¾oz) Fairtrade cocoa
50g (1¾oz) Fairtrade plain chocolate, chopped
2 fresh Fairtrade pears, peeled, cored, and chopped
150ml (5fl oz) milk

## METHOD

**Preheat** the oven to 180°C/350°F/Gas Mark 4. Base-line an 18cm (7in) springform cake tin and grease the sides with butter.

**Cream** the fat with the sugar until light and fluffy.

**Beat** the eggs in gradually, adding a little of the flour each time.

**Fold** in the cocoa, chopped chocolate, and pears. Add the milk to the mixture and combine.

**Pour** the batter into the prepared cake tin, place it in the oven, and bake for about 30 minutes.

*Tip* This is nice served cold. Dust the cake with icing sugar to finish.

# CHOCOLATE AND PEARS MAKE A HEAVENLY COUPLE

**Veronica Piekosz** from Great Smeaton, Yorkshire

# MARMA-BANANA CRUNCHIES

## INGREDIENTS

Makes 12 slices
Preparation time 5 minutes
Cooking time 35–40 minutes, plus
5 minutes cooling

50g (1¾oz) caster sugar
100g (3½oz) butter, softened
1 ripe Fairtrade banana, mashed
50g (1¾oz) Fairtrade mixed dried fruit

1 heaped tbsp Fairtrade medium-cut
marmalade
100g (3½oz) plain flour
50g (1¾oz) ground rice
75g (2½oz) porridge oats
1 tbsp Fairtrade Demerara sugar to
sprinkle on top of mixture before
baking

## METHOD

**Preheat** the oven to 190°C/375°F/Gas Mark 5. Grease a 15 x 30cm (6 x 12in) shallow baking tin with butter and line it with a strip of greaseproof paper.

**Cream** together the sugar and butter in a large bowl with an electric beater until smooth and creamy.

**Add** the banana, mixed fruit, and marmalade, and beat well.

**Mix** the flour, rice, and oats together in another bowl before adding them to the creamed mixture.

**Combine** well and pour into the prepared tin. Sprinkle with the Demerara sugar.

**Bake** for 35–40 minutes or until golden brown and set.

**Mark** into 12 slices with a knife, and allow to cool in the tin for 5 minutes before turning out.

**Cool** on a rack before cutting. Enjoy!

*Tip* If you have trouble finding ground rice, just use plain flour.

**Sally Hill** from Brighton

# CHOCOLATE AND BEETROOT LITTLE FANCIES

## INGREDIENTS

Makes about 24 little cakes
Preparation time 30 minutes
Cooking time 10-15 minutes

60g (1¾oz) Fairtrade cocoa
180g (6½oz) plain flour
2 tsp baking powder
230g (8oz) caster sugar
2 tsp baking powder

230g (8oz) beetroot, cooked
1 tsp Fairtrade vanilla extract or Fairtrade
  vanilla seeds
3 large eggs
200ml (7fl oz) vegetable oil or corn oil
A little zest from a Fairtrade orange
40g (1½oz) Fairtrade plain chocolate,
  grated

## METHOD

**Preheat** the oven to 180°C/350°F/Gas Mark 4. Place 24 fairy cake paper cases into the cups of two 12-hole muffin tins.

**Sift** the cocoa, flour, and baking powder into a large bowl. Add the sugar and combine.

**Whizz** the cooked beetroot, vanilla, eggs, and oil in a food processor, or use a hand blender.

**Mix** the wet ingredients into the dry.

**Add** the zest and grated chocolate.

**Spoon** the batter into the cases and place in the oven.

**Bake** for 10-15 minutes.

**Mrs S Davis** from Worcester Park, Surrey

# INDIAN SPICED VANILLA CHAI

## INGREDIENTS

Serves 4-6
Preparation time 5-10 minutes;
Cooking time 10 minutes

2 tsp Fairtrade black pepper
2 tsp grated fresh root ginger

6 Fairtrade cardamom pods
25cm (10in) Fairtrade cinnamon stick
3 tsp Fairtrade cloves
3 Fairtrade tea bags or 2 tbsp Fairtrade loose tea
1 Fairtrade vanilla pod, seeds only

## METHOD

**Crush** the black pepper, ginger root, cardamom pods, cinnamon stick, and cloves together.

**Pour** 8 cups of water into a saucepan and add the crushed spices and tea bags (or loose tea), along with the seeds from the vanilla pod.

**Bring** to a boil and cook over a medium heat for 10 minutes.

**Strain** the chai to remove the spices and prevent the tea becoming too strong. Serve in cups.

*Tip* You can serve each cup of chai with a cinnamon stick for decoration.

# CHOCOLATE, CHERRY, AND COCONUT SLICE

## INGREDIENTS

Serves 8–10
Preparation time 20 minutes plus chilling
No cooking

225g (8oz) Fairtrade dark chocolate
225g (8oz) butter
75ml (2½fl oz) Fairtrade strong coffee

2 large eggs
50g (1¾oz) caster sugar
225g (8oz) digestive biscuits, roughly crushed into large chunks
100g (3½oz) natural glacé cherries, halved
50g (1¾oz) desiccated coconut

## METHOD

**Line** a 900g (2lb) loaf tin with a double layer of clingfilm, leaving enough over the edges to fold over the top later.

**Place** the chocolate, butter, and coffee together in a saucepan and melt over a low heat, stirring occasionally until smooth.

**Whisk** together the eggs and sugar in a medium bowl.

**Put** the crushed biscuits into another large bowl and mix in the cherries and coconut.

**Tip** the egg mixture over the biscuits, then the melted chocolate, and stir thoroughly until blended.

**Pour** the mixture into loaf tin, smooth over the surface, cover with the excess cling film, and when cold chill overnight in the fridge.

**Slice** and serve on its own or with whipped double cream and a dusting of cocoa powder.

*Tip* Easy to make, and it can be prepared ahead of time. This will be well received whether served with a cup of tea in the afternoon or with a dessert wine at a dinner party.

**Judges' note** This is a fabulously rich and decadent recipe that we will definitely be making again.

**Mrs Val Pendleton** from Brackley, Northamptonshire

# FRUIT AND NUT FLIP-FLAPS

## INGREDIENTS

Makes 18
Preparation time 5 minutes
Cooking time 30–35 minutes

125g (4½oz) butter, or margarine, plus a
    little for greasing
225g (8oz) Fairtrade sugar (any variety)

5 tbsp Fairtrade honey
350g (12oz) Fairtrade muesli
125g (4½oz) wholemeal flour
150g (5½oz) Fairtrade dried apricots,
    chopped
60g (2oz) walnuts, chopped
2 medium eggs, beaten

## METHOD

**Preheat** the oven to 180°C/350°F/Gas Mark 4. Grease a 20 x 30cm (8 x 12in) baking tin with butter.
Line it with a strip of greaseproof paper and set it aside.

**Place** the butter, sugar, and honey in a small pan, and melt slowly until runny.

**Put** all the remaining ingredients in a large bowl meanwhile and make a well in the centre.

**Pour** the beaten eggs and melted butter mixture into the centre and mix well.

**Press** the mixture into the prepared tin and bake in the preheated oven for 30–35 minutes until it is
golden brown.

**Allow** to cool completely before turning out and cutting.

*Tip* These store well in an airtight container for up to four days.

# IMAGINE: SOMETHING SWEET YET GOOD FOR YOU TOO

**Jenifer Whyler** from Dyserth, Wales

# ANZAC BISCUITS

## INGREDIENTS

Makes about 24 large biscuits
Preparation time: 20 minutes
Cooking time 15-20 minutes

100g (3½oz) rolled oats
100g (3½oz) flaked coconut

100g (3½oz) Fairtrade Demerara sugar
100g (3½oz) plain flour
120g (4oz) butter
2 tbsp Fairtrade golden syrup
1 level tsp bicarbonate of soda

## METHOD

**Preheat** the oven to 150°C/300°F/Gas Mark 2. Grease two baking trays and set them aside.

**Mix** together the dry ingredients in a big bowl.

**Melt** the butter with 15ml (1tbsp) boiling water, add the syrup, and heat gently in a saucepan.

**Add** the bicarbonate of soda once it is all nice and runny. When it froths up, pour it over the dry ingredients and mix thoroughly.

**Take** one tablespoon of the mixture at a time and roll it into a ball in the palms of your (clean) hands.

**Place** each one on a baking tray and flatten out until cookie thickness

**Bake** in the oven for about 15-20 minutes. Keep an eye on the biscuits as the golden syrup can burn quickly.

**Let** them cool completely on the tray before lifting them off.

*Tip* Fairtrade fanatics might want to substitute runny honey for the golden syrup. This will cause delicious variations in flavour as many organic honeys differ from year to year.

**Kirsty Jackman** from St Cuthbert's Catholic Community College, Merseyside

# APPLE AND SULTANA CAKE

## INGREDIENTS

Serves 8-10
Preparation time: 30 minutes;
Cooking time: 35-40 minutes

115g (4oz) butter or hard margarine,
  plus extra for greasing
175g (6oz) Fairtrade sultanas
115g (4oz) Fairtrade soft brown sugar
100ml (3½fl oz) Fairtrade apple juice

225g (8oz) self-raising flour
1 tsp baking powder
5 tsp Fairtrade ground cinnamon
3 medium-sized Fairtrade eating apples
  unpeeled, cored, and cut in to 1cm
  (½in) chunks
2 large eggs, beaten
Icing sugar for dusting

## METHOD

**Preheat** the oven to 160°C/325°F/Gas Mark 3. Grease and line a 20cm (8in) round cake tin.

**Melt** the butter or margarine in a large saucepan.

**Add** the sultanas, sugar, and apple juice and stir for a few minutes over a medium heat. Remove from the heat and allow to cool.

**Sift** together the flour, baking powder, and 4 tsp of the cinnamon in a bowl and set aside.

**Sprinkle** the apple chunks with the remaining cinnamon and stir them into the flour mixture. Stir in the eggs and combine.

**Add** this to the melted mixture and stir well.

**Transfer** the mixture into the cake tin and place it in the oven.

**Bake** for 35-40 minutes until a skewer inserted comes out clean.

**Cool** in the tin for 5 minutes, then turn out on to a wire rack and dust with icing sugar.

**Judges' note** This fantastic cake is so moist it would double as a pudding. It's a perfect family cake as it will keep for a few days in an airtight tin, getting better and better as time passes.

**Miss C A Mason** from London

# TOFFEE BROWNIES

## INGREDIENTS

Makes 18 squares
Preparation time 30 minutes
Cooking time 40-45 minutes

100g (3½oz) Fairtrade dark chocolate
175g (6oz) butter
5 tbsp double cream
350g (12oz) caster sugar
4 large eggs

2 tsp Fairtrade vanilla extract
200g (7oz) plain flour
1 tsp baking powder
100g (3½oz) packet pecans, roughly chopped
205g (7¼oz) creamy Fairtrade toffees
50g (1¾oz) Fairtrade dark chocolate, to decorate

## METHOD

**Preheat** the oven to 180°C/350°F/Gas Mark 4. Line a 28 x 18cm (11 x 7in) shallow baking tin with baking parchment.

**Break** up the 100g (3½oz) chocolate in a roomy bowl and add the butter. Sit the bowl over a pan of simmering water, stirring occasionally until the chocolate has melted. Take off the heat.

**Stir** the sugar into the melted chocolate mixture.

**Lightly** beat the eggs with the vanilla, and then stir them in to the chocolate mixture.

**Sift** in the flour and baking powder, mixing lightly. Then stir in the pecans.

**Put** the toffees and the cream in a pan. Place over a gentle heat to melt, stirring all the time.

**Pour** half the chocolate mixture into the tin and drizzle over three-quarters of the toffee sauce. Spread over the rest of the chocolate mixture and place in the oven for 40-45 minutes until firm to the touch.

**Leave** the brownies to cool in the tin for 20 minutes, and then turn them out. Peel away the baking parchment, and cool on a wire rack.

**Decorate** the brownies by reheating the remaining toffee. Melt the 50g (1¾oz) of chocolate in a separate bowl over simmering water. Drizzle the toffee over the brownie, followed by the melted chocolate, using the tip of a teaspoon.

**Judges' note** This would be perfect for a children's party.

**Catherine Hughes** from St Cuthbert's Catholic Community College, Merseyside

# CHOCOLATE ORANGE TEALOAF

## INGREDIENTS

Makes one 900g (2lb) loaf
Preparation time 20 minutes plus a
few hours' soaking time
Cooking time 1½hours

150g (5½oz) Fairtrade golden
  granulated sugar
115g (4oz) Fairtrade raisins
115g (4oz) Fairtrade sultanas

55g (2oz) Fairtrade dried apricots,
  chopped
Grated rind of 2 Fairtrade oranges
300ml (10fl oz) hot Fairtrade tea
275g (10oz) self-raising flour
55g (2oz) Fairtrade plain chocolate,
  chopped into small pieces
1 large egg, lightly beaten

## METHOD

**Place** the sugar, fruit, and grated rind in a bowl and cover with the hot tea.

**Stir** everything together, cover and leave to stand for a few hours so the fruit absorbs the tea.

**Preheat** the oven to 150°C/300°F/Gas Mark 2 when the fruit has finished soaking. Line a 900g (2lb) loaf tin with baking parchment and set it aside.

**Stir** the flour into the fruit, add the chocolate pieces and egg, and mix thoroughly.

**Spoon** the mixture into the loaf tin and bake for approximately 1½hours.

**Insert** a skewer into the centre of the loaf towards the end of the baking time. If it fails to come out clean, give it a few more minutes to cook.

**Turn** the loaf out, remove the paper, and leave it to cool on a rack.

**Mrs Diane Boden** from Putney, London

# BANANA AND NUT FINGERS

## INGREDIENTS

Makes 12
Preparation time 10 minutes
Cooking time 20-25 minutes plus
cooling

225g (8oz) butter, plus extra for greasing
225g (8oz) Fairtrade sugar
2 large eggs

225g (8oz) wholemeal flour
225g (8oz) porridge oats
½tsp bicarbonate of soda
4 ripe Fairtrade bananas, peeled
   and sliced
50g (1¾oz) mixed Fairtrade nuts

## METHOD

**Preheat** oven to 190°C/375°F/Gas Mark 5. Grease a 23cm (9in) square tin with butter. Line it with a strip of greaseproof paper and set it aside.

**Cream** the butter and sugar in a bowl using an electric beater until smooth and creamy.

**Add** the eggs one by one, beating well after each addition.

**Fold** in the dry ingredients and spread half the mixture into the prepared tin.

**Cover** the mixture with the sliced bananas and nuts.

**Spread** the remaining mixture on top and bake for 20-25 minutes or until golden brown.

**Allow** to cool in the tin for 5 minutes before turning out and cutting into fingers. Eat warm or store in an airtight container. Enjoy!

# STAYS MOIST FOR SEVERAL DAYS BEFORE SERVING

**Mrs G Corbitt** from Nunthorpe, Middlesbrough

# APRICOT MUFFINS

## INGREDIENTS

Makes 12
Preparation time 20 minutes
Cooking time 15 minutes

300g (10oz) plain flour
1 tbsp baking powder
½tsp Fairtrade mixed spice
150g (5½oz) Fairtrade dried apricots,
   chopped

85g (3oz) Fairtrade soft brown sugar
50g (1¾oz) chopped nuts
1 tsp grated rind of a Fairtrade orange
125g (4½oz) butter, melted
200ml (7fl oz) milk
1 large egg, lightly beaten

## METHOD

**Preheat** the oven to 200°C/400°F/Gas Mark 6. Brush a muffin tin with oil and set it aside.

**Sift** the flour, baking powder, and mixed spice into a large bowl.

**Stir** in the apricots, sugar, nuts, and rind and set aside.

**Whisk** together the butter, milk, and beaten egg. Make a well in the centre of the dry ingredients and add the egg mixture.

**Mix** lightly until just combined and spoon into the prepared muffin tin.

**Place** in the oven and bake 15 minutes or until golden.

**Loosen** the muffins with a spatula and turn them out onto a cooling rack.

*Tip* You could use Fairtrade brazil nuts in this recipe, to increase the number of Fairtrade ingredients.

# READY IN NO TIME WHEN YOU NEED SOMETHING SWEET

**Grace Wells** from Lurgan, County Armagh

# A TASTE OF THE CARIBBEAN BANANA BREAD

## INGREDIENTS

Makes one 900g (2lb) loaf
Preparation time 25 minutes
Cooking time 45 minutes

Vegetable oil for brushing
250g (9oz) self-raising flour
1 tsp baking powder
1 tsp Fairtrade mixed spice
80g (3oz) hard margarine or butter

3 medium Fairtrade bananas, mashed
3 large eggs
80g (3oz) plus 1 tbsp Fairtrade golden
    granulated sugar
3 tbsp Fairtrade clear honey
40g (1½oz) dried Fairtrade pineapple,
    chopped
3 tbsp plus 1 tbsp desiccated coconut

## METHOD

**Preheat** the oven to 180°C/350°F/Gas Mark 4. Line a 900g (2lb) loaf tin with greaseproof paper and then brush on some oil and set it aside.

**Sift** the flour, baking powder, and mixed spice into a bowl and rub in the margarine or butter until the mixture resembles breadcrumbs.

**Stir** the mashed bananas into the mixture along with the eggs. Mix well and then add the 80g (3oz) of the sugar and the honey.

**Stir** until smooth and then add the pineapple and 3 tbsp of the coconut and combine.

**Spoon** into the loaf tin and sprinkle the remaining tbsp each of sugar and coconut on top of the mixture.

**Place** into the oven for about 45 minutes until the top is springy with a lovely crunchy topping, and a skewer inserted into the bread comes out clean.

**Remove** the loaf from the tin once it has cooled, peel off the paper, and place on a cooling rack.

**Vicki Partridge** from Stanford-le-Hope, Essex

# NUTTY "DROP" BUNS

## INGREDIENTS

Makes about 12 buns
Preparation time 15 minutes
Cooking time 10–12 minutes

120g (4oz) butter
170g (6oz) self-raising flour
60g (2oz) semolina or ground rice
85g (3oz) Fairtrade golden granulated sugar

120g (4oz) Fairtrade dates, finely chopped
60g (2oz) walnuts, chopped
2 large eggs, beaten
1 tsp Fairtrade vanilla extract

### Topping
1 tbsp Fairtrade coffee granules
120g (4oz) golden icing sugar

## METHOD

**Preheat** the oven to 190°C/375°F/Gas Mark 5.

**Rub** the butter into the flour and semolina or ground rice in a large bowl.

**Add** the sugar, dates, and walnuts and combine.

**Pour** in the eggs and vanilla extract and mix to a stiff consistency.

**Divide** the mixture between 12 holes of a non-stick patty tin (the sort you would make fairy cakes in).

**Bake** towards the top of the oven for approximately 10–12 minutes.

**Leave** the buns to cool. Make the icing by blending the coffee granules with 1 tbsp of boiling water. Then blend the coffee liquid with the icing sugar until the icing reaches drizzling consistency. Top each bun with icing and half a walnut, then leave to set.

*Tip* Eat these on the day you make them. They are great for lunchboxes or an after-school treat.

# A SATISFYING TREAT FOR ANY OCCASION

**Mrs Pat Ayres MBE** from Kemble, Gloucestershire

# APRICOT AND OAT SQUARES

## INGREDIENTS

Makes 18
Preparation time 10 minutes
Cooking time 35 minutes

250g (9oz) Fairtrade dried apricots,
   chopped
180g (6oz) unsalted butter, diced
125g (4½oz) Fairtrade golden
   granulated sugar

2 tbsp Fairtrade honey
300g (10½oz) plain flour
150g (5oz) porridge oats
30g (1oz) Fairtrade sesame seeds
2 tsp Fairtrade ground ginger
30g (1oz) Fairtrade brazil nuts, chopped

## METHOD

**Simmer** the chopped apricots for about 15-20 minutes in 100ml (3½oz) water until soft. Preheat the oven to 200°C/400°F/Gas Mark 6.

**Grease** a square or oblong 16 x 25cm (6 x 10in) cake tin. Line it with parchment and set it aside.

**Melt** the butter, sugar, and honey slowly in a saucepan until they are runny.

**Put** the flour, oats, sesame seeds, and ginger in a bowl and stir in the chopped brazil nuts.

**Pour** the melted butter mixture into the centre of the dry ingredients and stir well.

**Press** half the mixture into a tin, spread on the apricots, and press the rest of the mixture on top.

**Place** in the oven and cook for 30-35 minutes.

**Leave** to cool in the tin for about 15 minutes, and then cut into squares.

*Tip* You may find it easiest to chop the apricots using scissors. This is nice for lunchboxes, or served warm as a pudding with Ben & Jerry's Fairtrade vanilla ice cream.

**Christine Bleathman** from London

# STICKY BANANA FINGERS

## INGREDIENTS

Makes 18
Preparation time 10 minutes
Cooking time 25-30 minutes

150g (5½oz) walnuts, roughly chopped
4 large, ripe Fairtrade bananas
220g (8oz) wholemeal flour
1 heaped tsp baking powder

1 tsp Fairtrade ground cinnamon
175g (6oz) Fairtrade soft brown sugar
Zest of 1 Fairtrade lemon, finely grated
Zest of 1 Fairtrade orange, finely grated
110g (4oz) butter, softened
2 large eggs, at room temperature,
  beaten

## METHOD

**Preheat** oven to 180°C/350°F/Gas Mark 4. Grease a 16 x 26cm (6 x 10in) baking tin with butter. Line with a strip of greaseproof paper and set aside.

**Place** the walnuts on a baking sheet and toast in the oven for 5-6 minutes. Remove from the oven and leave to cool.

**Mash** three of the bananas meanwhile, and chop the remaining one into 1cm (½in) chunks. Set aside.

**Sift** together the dry ingredients into the bowl of an electric mixer, adding back any retained bran from the wholemeal flour.

**Add** all the remaining ingredients except for the chopped bananas and walnuts and beat well until smooth. If the mixture looks a little stiff, add some milk, a teaspoon at a time, to soften it so that it drops easily off a spoon.

**Lightly** fold in the chopped banana and walnuts. Pour the mixture into the prepared tin.

**Bake** for 25-30 minutes until golden brown and set.

**Allow** to cool in the tin completely before cutting.

**Francesca Lavell** from Marist Convent School, Sunninghill, Berkshire

# SMOOTH OASIS

## INGREDIENTS

Serves 4
Preparation time 25 minutes
Cooking time 1-2 minutes

4 large figs
250g (9oz) mascarpone cheese
1 large egg, beaten, for dipping
2 tbsp milk, for dipping

1-2 tbsp flour, for rolling
8 tbsp breadcrumbs, for rolling
200g (7oz) Fairtrade dark chocolate
125ml (4½fl oz) single cream
Sunflower oil for deep-frying
4 scoops Fairtrade vanilla ice cream

## METHOD

**Wash** and peel the figs and cut them in half. Scoop the insides out, reserving the shells. Place the fig pulp into a bowl.

**Add** the mascarpone cheese to the fig pulp, and mix them together.

**Place** the mixture back into the fig shells and close them together

**Mix** the egg and milk together in a bowl.

**Roll** each fig in the flour and dip them into the egg and milk mixture. Then roll them in the bread crumbs. Place them on a plate and set aside.

**Melt** the chocolate gently in a bowl over a pan of boiling water.

**Add** the cream once the chocolate has melted, stirring it in gently until it reaches a smooth consistency. Set it aside.

**Use** a deep-fat fryer to heat the sunflower oil until it is hot enough to brown a cube of bread in 1 minute. Take the figs and deep-fry them for 1 minute or until crisp and golden brown.

**Place** a scoop of ice cream on each of four plates. Then set a deep-fried fig on top of the ice cream. Gently drizzle the chocolate sauce over and serve.

**Nora Asselah,** from Birmingham

# RICH CHOCOLATE AND COCONUT PUDDING

## INGREDIENTS

Serves 4 slightly greedy chocoholics
Preparation time 5 minutes
Cooking time 15 minutes

125g (4½oz) quinoa flakes or Fairtrade quinoa

30g (1oz) Fairtrade cocoa

30g (1oz) Fairtrade granulated sugar
35g (1¼ oz) Fairtrade dark chocolate
115g (4oz) Fairtrade honey
50g (1¾oz) sachet creamed coconut
1 tsp Fairtrade vanilla extract
1 small Fairtrade banana to serve, sliced

## METHOD

**Place** the quinoa flakes, cocoa powder, and sugar in a saucepan with 300 ml (10fl oz) water and cook slowly over a low heat, stirring occasionally, for about 10–15 minutes, until thick.

**Break** up 25g (1oz) of the chocolate into squares, grate the rest in a separate dish, and set both aside. Remove the quinoa from the heat and stir in the chocolate squares, honey, creamed coconut, and the vanilla extract.

**Stir** until the chocolate and coconut have melted.

**Leave** to cool, and then divide into glass bowls.

**Chill** thoroughly overnight to set. To serve, top with banana slices and sprinkle with the grated chocolate.

*Tip* If you have difficulty finding quinoa flakes in the shops you can order them online. See page 219 for more information.

# A PUDDING FOR SLIGHTLY GREEDY CHOCOHOLICS

**Mrs Linda Perkins** from Chelmsford

# ESPRESSO AND HAZELNUT CAKE

## Rose Gray and Ruth Rogers

We make a delicious coffee, chocolate, and hazelnut cake, normally with instant coffee, but we have decided to switch to using a Fairtrade espresso coffee in the cake now, and we are thrilled with the result. Salute to Fairtrade.

## INGREDIENTS

Serves 6
Preparation time 20 minutes
Cooking time 50 minutes

200g (7oz) butter, plus extra for greasing
400g (14oz) hazelnuts, shelled
2 tbsp espresso used making Fairtrade coffee

200g (7oz) Fairtrade 70% dark chocolate, broken into small pieces
6 medium eggs
220g (7¾oz) caster sugar

## METHOD

**Preheat** the oven to 190°C/375°F/Gas Mark 5.

**Using** extra butter, grease a 25cm (10in) cake tin, and line with parchment paper.

**Roast** the hazelnuts in the oven until brown. Let cool, rub off the skins, and grind the nuts to a fine powder.

**Make** up espresso, using Fairtrade coffee.

**Melt** the chocolate with the butter and coffee in a bowl over barely simmering water. Cool, then fold in the hazelnuts.

**Separate** the eggs and beat the yolks and sugar in a mixer until pale and doubled in size. Fold in the chocolate.

**Beat** the egg whites until stiff, and then carefully fold into the mixture. Pour into the tin.

**Bake** in the oven for 50 minutes. Cool in the tin.

*Tip* Turn the cake upside down out of the tin to serve. You could dust it with some icing sugar it you like.

# THE ULTIMATE ENERGY BAR

## INGREDIENTS

Makes 18
Preparation time 10 minutes
Cooking time 25 minutes

50g (1¾oz) unsalted butter, diced
40g (1½oz) Fairtrade golden granulated
  sugar
3 tbsp Fairtrade honey
1 large Fairtrade banana, mashed
150g (5½oz) organic porridge oats

3 tbsp organic pumpkin seeds
3 tbsp organic Fairtrade sesame seeds
30g (1oz) Fairtrade brazil nuts, chopped
60g (2oz) Fairtrade dried mango or
  apricots, chopped

Optional topping
100g (3½oz) Fairtrade dark chocolate,
  broken into pieces

## METHOD

**Preheat** the oven to 180°C/350°F/Gas Mark 4. Grease a 16 x 26cm (6 x 10in) baking tin with butter. Line with a strip of greaseproof paper and set aside.

**Place** the butter, sugar, and honey in a small pan, and melt slowly until runny. Then mix in the mashed banana.

**Put** all the remaining ingredients into a large bowl and make a well in the centre.

**Pour** the melted butter mixture into the centre and combine.

**Press** the mixture into the prepared tin and bake in the oven for 20 minutes until firm and the edges are turning golden brown.

**Allow** to cool in the tin for 5 minutes. Turn out, peel off the baking parchment and cut into bars.

**Melt** the chocolate carefully in a bowl placed over a pan of simmering water. Drizzle it over the cooled bars and allow it to set. Store in an airtight container once cool.

**Henrietta Lampkin** from London

# TAKES THE BISCUIT!

## INGREDIENTS

Makes 18 squares or 36 bite-sized pieces
Preparation time 10 minutes

250g (9oz) Fairtrade dark chocolate, chopped
125g (4½oz) unsalted butter, diced

397g (14oz) can condensed milk
360g (12½oz) ginger biscuits, crushed
50g (1¾oz) Fairtrade raisins
90g (3oz, or about 4 lumps) stem ginger, finely chopped
3 tbsp stem ginger syrup

## METHOD

**Line** a 22 x 30cm (9 x 12in) tin with cling film.

**Slowly** melt together the chocolate, butter, and condensed milk in a large pan on a low heat. Mix well.

**Add** the other ingredients and combine thoroughly.

**Pour** into the baking tin and level out the mixture.

**Place** in the fridge and leave there until set.

*Tip* Serve these in bite-sized pieces. This recipe is very, very rich and indulgent, and will satisfy when you need a serious chocolate hit.

# SO RICH AND INDULGENT, JUST A MORSEL WILL DO

**Mrs Sue Sherman** from Winwick, Northampton

# BANANA, WALNUT, AND ORANGE LOAF

## INGREDIENTS

Makes one 900g (2lb) loaf
Preparation time 20 minutes
Cooking time 1 hour

175g (6oz) walnuts
4 medium Fairtrade bananas
115g (4oz) plain flour
115g (4oz) wholemeal flour

1 rounded tsp baking powder
1 tsp Fairtrade ground cinnamon
Grated zest of 1 Fairtrade orange
115g (4oz) butter at room temperature
175g (6oz) Fairtrade soft brown sugar
2 large eggs at room temperature

## METHOD

**Preheat** the oven to 180°C/350°F/Gas Mark 4. Lightly butter a 900g (2lb) loaf tin and set it aside.

**Spread** the walnuts on a baking sheet. As soon as the oven is ready, place the walnuts in the oven and toast them lightly.

**Remove** them from the oven after 7–8 minutes and leave them to cool down on a chopping board. Then chop them fairly roughly.

**Peel** and mash three of the bananas to a purée in a bowl with a fork. Then peel and chop the fourth banana into slices of about 1cm (½in) each. Set the bananas aside.

**Sift** both of the flours, the baking powder, and the cinnamon in a large mixing bowl, holding the sieve up high so the ingredients get a good airing.

**Add** the rest of the ingredients, apart from the bananas and walnuts, and use an electric hand whisk to beat the mixture smoothly, first on a low speed and then on a high.

**Fold** the chopped walnuts and bananas in lightly. If the resulting mixture does not drop off a spoon easily, add a few drops of milk to bind the mixture.

**Pile** the mixture into the prepared tin and level out with a spoon. If you want a fine crisp touch to the top, sprinkle over a little sugar.

**Place** in the centre of the oven and bake for about 1 hour. Let it cool for about 5 minutes and then turn it out onto a cooling rack, allowing it to go completely cold before serving.

**Olivia Harris** from Marist Convent School, Sunninghill, Berkshire

# STICKY BANOFFEE MUFFINS

## INGREDIENTS

Makes 10
Preparation time 20 minutes
Cooking time 20 minutes

125g (4½oz) Fairtrade dried dates, chopped
3 tsp Fairtrade instant coffee granules
1½tsp bicarbonate of soda
300g (10oz) self-raising flour

½tsp salt
100g (3½oz) Fairtrade golden granulated sugar
1 egg, beaten
100ml (3½oz) oil
1 large very ripe Fairtrade banana weighing 200g (7oz) peeled and mashed
3 tbsp ready-made toffee sauce

## METHOD

**Preheat** the oven to 190°C/375°F/Gas Mark 5. Line 10 holes of a muffin tin with muffin cases.

**Place** the chopped dates in a saucepan. Add the coffee granules, 1 tsp of the bicarbonate of soda and 200ml (7oz) of cold water.

**Bring** to the boil and simmer gently until a pulpy mixture is formed. Remove the pan from the heat to cool.

**Place** the dry ingredients, including the remaining bicarbonate of soda, in a large bowl and stir to mix

**Mix** the beaten egg with the oil and the mashed banana.

**Add** the wet ingredients to the dry and mix gently but thoroughly with a fork.

**Divide** the mixture evenly between the muffin cases.

**Bake** for 20 minutes until the muffins are browned, risen, and springy to the touch. Remove from the oven and place on a cooling rack.

**Brush** the tops of the muffins with the toffee sauce while they are still hot.

**Serve** as they are, or with custard or cream for a delicious dessert.

**Mrs J Coldicott** from Bexley, Kent

# TRINIDADIAN COCONUT SWEETBREAD

## INGREDIENTS

Makes one 900g (2lb) loaf
Preparation time 20 minutes
Cooking time 1–1¼ hours

225g (8oz) plain flour
3 tsp baking powder
1 tsp salt
1 tbsp Fairtrade mixed spice

180g (6½oz) Fairtrade golden
  granulated sugar (plus 2 tbsp extra
  for dusting)
225g (8oz) desiccated coconut
2 large eggs
200ml (7fl oz) coconut milk
125g (4½oz) butter, very soft
175g (6oz) Fairtrade mixed dried fruit

## METHOD

**Preheat** the oven to 160°C/325°F/Gas Mark 3. Grease a 900g (2lb) loaf tin. Line it with baking parchment and set it aside.

**Sift** the flour, baking powder, salt, and mixed spice together in a mixing bowl. Add the sugar and coconut and stir to combine.

**Make** a well in the centre of the ingredients and add the eggs, coconut milk, and very soft butter.

**Add** the mixed dried fruit and stir the batter just until all the ingredients are combined.

**Pour** into the prepared loaf tin. Level the top and dust with the 2 tbsp sugar.

**Place** in the oven. After an hour test if it is done by placing a skewer into the loaf. If it comes out clean the loaf is done. If not, continue baking and check again after 15 minutes.

**Turn** out of the tin and leave to cool on a baking rack.

*Tip* This highly crumbly, irresistible sweetbread is often better the following day as the flavours tend to develop more. Make sure you use salted butter for this recipe as it adds to the flavour.

**Melanie Lewis** from Hillingdon, Uxbridge

# BANANA AND DATE LOAF

## INGREDIENTS

Makes one 900g (2lb) loaf
Preparation time 1 hour soaking plus
20 minutes
Cooking time 1 hour

125g (4½oz) Fairtrade dates
1 large Fairtrade banana, peeled
150g (5½oz) butter or margarine

75g (2½oz) Fairtrade golden granulated
  sugar
110g (4oz) gram flour
1 tsp baking powder (gluten-free)
110g (4oz) brown rice flour
50g (1¾oz) ground almonds
100g (3½oz) Fairtrade plain chocolate

## METHOD

**Place** dates in a bowl. Cover them with boiling water and let them soak for an hour. After soaking the dates, preheat the oven to 160°C/325°F/Gas Mark 3. Grease a 900g (2lb) loaf tin, line it with parchment paper, and set it aside.

**Drain** the excess liquid from the soaked dates. Purée them with the banana and set aside.

**Melt** the butter or margarine and sugar in a saucepan over a medium heat and set aside.

**Mix** the gram flour, baking powder, brown rice flour, and ground almonds together in a large bowl. Add the fruit purée and the melted butter mixture and combine well.

**Pour** the batter into the prepared loaf tin and bake for approximately 60 minutes, or until an inserted skewer comes out clean.

**Remove** the loaf from the oven when it is cooked and let it cool. Meanwhile melt the chocolate in a bowl placed over a barely simmering saucepan of water. When the loaf has cooled, smother it in the melted chocolate.

*Tip* This recipe works equally well using regular rice flour instead of brown. You could also use milk chocolate instead of plain if you prefer. This is an excellent recipe for coeliac sufferers.

**Heather Raisin** from Quorn, Leicestershire

# RASPBERRY FLAPJACKS

## INGREDIENTS

Makes 18
Preparation time 10 minutes
Cooking time 30 minutes

125g (4½oz) raspberries
250g (9oz) butter, diced, plus extra
    for greasing
1 tbsp golden syrup or Fairtrade honey

1 tsp bicarbonate of soda
1 tsp baking powder
250g (9oz) porridge oats
200g (7oz) plain flour
100g (3½oz) desiccated coconut
100g (3½oz) Fairtrade brown sugar

## METHOD

**Preheat** the oven to 180°C /350°F/Gas Mark 4. Grease a deep baking tin measuring 16 x 25cm (6 x 10in) with butter. Line it with a strip of greaseproof paper and set it aside.

**Crush** the raspberries in a small bowl.

**Place** the butter and syrup or honey in a small pan, and melt together slowly until runny.

**Sprinkle** over the bicarbonate of soda and stir the mixture until it is frothy.

**Place** all the remaining ingredients in a large bowl and make a well in the centre.

**Pour** the melted butter mixture into the centre and mix well.

**Spread** half of the mixture into the tin, spread the raspberries over the top, and then cover with the remaining mixture.

**Place** in the oven and bake for 25 minutes until golden. Allow the flapjacks to cool before turning them out and cutting them into squares.

*Tip* You can also make these using frozen raspberries. Once they have thawed, break them up with a fork. Squeeze out any excess juice before using them.

**Sally Hickson** from Altrincham, Cheshire

# CHOCOLATE BRAZIL BANANA BREAD

## INGREDIENTS

Makes one 450g (1lb) loaf
Preparation time 30 minutes
Cooking time 45 minutes

2 large eggs
3 ripe Fairtrade bananas, peeled and
   mashed
1 tsp Fairtrade vanilla extract
50g (1¾oz) butter, melted, plus extra
   butter for greasing

100g (3½oz) Fairtrade brazil nuts,
   roughly chopped
45g (1½oz) Fairtrade chocolate, roughly
   chopped
200g (7oz) self-raising flour
Pinch of salt
100g (3½oz) Fairtrade golden
   granulated sugar
2 tsp baking powder

## METHOD

**Preheat** the oven to 170°C/325°F/Gas Mark 3.

**Line** a 450g (1lb) loaf tin with parchment paper.

**Whisk** the eggs with a fork in a large bowl until they are light and creamy. Add the mashed bananas and mix well.

**Add** the the remaining ingredients to the banana mixture and stir until well combined and moist.

**Tip** the mixture into the prepared loaf tin (using a spatula to scrape clean the sides of the mixing bowl) and bake for about 45 minutes or until well risen and golden brown. The loaf is cooked when you can insert a toothpick or skewer and it comes out clean.

**Cool** for about 10 minutes before tipping out onto a wire tray to cool completely.

**Slice** and serve.

**Karen Costello-McFeat,** from Eastbourne

# FAIRTRADE COOKIES

## INGREDIENTS

Makes 16
Preparation time 20 minutes
Cooking time 10-12 minutes

115g (4oz) butter, softened
115g (4oz) Fairtrade golden granulated
 sugar
1 large egg, beaten
1 tbsp wild blossom Fairtrade honey

175g (6oz) plain flour
100g (3½oz) Fairtrade milk chocolate,
 chopped
80g (3oz) Fairtrade dried apricots,
 chopped
1½ tbsp Fairtrade Fruit Passion juice,
 either orange, apple, or tropical

## METHOD

**Preheat** the oven to 180°C/350°F/Gas Mark 4. Grease two large baking sheets and set them aside.

**Cream** the butter and sugar together in a mixing bowl until light and fluffy.

**Beat** the egg in next, and stir in the honey.

**Sift** the flour into the mixture, add the chocolate and fruit, and mix it all in.

**Pour** in the fruit juice, stirring it in between each spoonful, until the mixture is a soft dropping consistency.

**Drop** tablespoonfuls of the mixture onto your baking sheets. Leave spaces between each spoonful so the cookies can spread easily.

**Bake** the cookies for 10 minutes (or until they are golden).

**Use** a spatula or palette knife to lift each cookie onto a cooling rack.

**Francesca Trewartha** from Radcliffe, Manchester

# FRUITY LOAF

## INGREDIENTS

Makes one 900g (2lb) loaf
Preparation time 40 minutes
including soaking time
Cooking time 45 minutes

1 Fairtrade teabag
125g (4½ oz) sultanas
125g (4½oz) Fairtrade dried apricots
2 tbsp Fairtrade honey

50g (1¾oz) Fairtrade golden granulated
  sugar
Fairtrade eating apple, peeled, cored,
  and grated
50g (1¾oz) walnuts
225g (8oz) self-raising wholemeal flour,
  sifted
1 tsp Fairtrade mixed spice
1 large egg, beaten

## METHOD

**Preheat** the oven to 180°C/350°F/Gas Mark 4. Line a 900g (2lb) loaf tin with baking parchment and set aside. Place the teabag in a bowl and add 150ml (5oz) boiling water. Leave for 3 minutes.

**Place** the dried fruit into another bowl. Remove the teabag from the tea and pour it over the fruit. Leave to soak for 30 minutes.

**Combine** the fruit and liquid with all the other ingredients, adding some milk if the mixture is dry.

**Spoon** the mixture into the prepared loaf tin, and level it off with a spoon.

**Place** the loaf in the oven and bake for 45 minutes. Test the loaf with a skewer until it comes out clean, allowing more time if required.

**Cool** the loaf for 10 minutes in the tin. Then remove it from the tin and leave it to cool further on the rack.

*Tip* This keeps several for days in a cake tin and becomes more moist, as do so many tealoaves, and it freezes well. You can also use Fairtrade brazil nuts in this recipe instead of the walnuts if you prefer.

**Mrs C J Davidson,** from Bacup, Lancashire

# MANGO AND BRAZIL NUT TEABREAD

## INGREDIENTS

Makes one 900g (2lb) loaf
Preparation time 20 minutes plus
overnight soaking
Cooking time 1 hour

100g (3½oz) Fairtrade dried mango, diced

90ml (3fl oz) Fairtrade tea for soaking the dried mango

125g (4½oz) butter, softened

125g (4½oz) Fairtrade golden granulated sugar

2 large eggs, beaten

250g (9oz) organic self-raising flour

50g (1¾oz) Fairtrade brazil nuts, chopped

2 tbsp maple syrup

100g (3½oz) Fairtrade fresh mango, diced

1 tsp Fairtrade mixed spice

## METHOD

**Soak** the dried mango overnight in the Fairtrade tea.

**Preheat** the oven to 160°C/325°F/Gas Mark 3. Grease a 900g (2lb) loaf tin, line it with parchment paper, and set it aside.

**Beat** together the butter and sugar until creamy and pale.

**Add** the beaten eggs and combine.

**Fold** in the flour, nuts, maple syrup, fresh mango, dried mango, any remaining tea, and the mixed spice.

**Pour** the mixture into the lined tin and place in the oven. Bake for 1 hour or until a skewer pierced in to the cake comes out clean.

**Cool** on a wire rack.

*Tip* This is delicious spread with unsalted butter.

**Judges' note** This loaf has lots of Fairtrade ingredients. It is a great variation on the teabread theme and it went down a storm in the office of the Fairtrade Foundation.

**David Naylor** from Barton, Oxford

# TEABREAD

## INGREDIENTS

Makes three 450g (1lb) loaves
Preparation time 10 minutes plus
overnight soaking time
Cooking time 50–55 minutes

450g (1lb) Fairtrade mixed dried fruit
225g (8oz) Fairtrade soft brown sugar
225ml (8fl oz) hot Fairtrade tea
450g (1lb) self-raising flour

55g (2oz) chopped almonds or walnuts
115g (4oz) glacé cherries, chopped
1 level tsp Fairtrade mixed spice
½ tsp Fairtrade ground cinnamon
Grating of nutmeg
3 medium eggs
2 tbsp brandy (optional)

## METHOD

**Soak** the fruit and sugar in the hot tea overnight.

**Preheat** the oven to 160°C/325°F/Gas Mark 3. Line three 450g (1lb) loaf tins with parchment paper. Place all the dry ingredients in a large bowl, add the soaked fruit, and combine.

**Add** the eggs and brandy, if using. Mix thoroughly and pour into the three prepared tins.

**Place** in the oven and bake for 50–55 minutes.

*Tip* You can also substitute 155g (5½oz) chopped dates for the mixed fruit. To make a slightly moister teabread, replace 55g (2oz) of sugar with 2 tbsp of malt extract. These loaves taste lovely with honey brushed on top, and they freeze very well.

# A COMFORTING AND WHOLESOME FAIR TREAT

**Mrs M Benn** from Ravensthorpe, Northamptonshire

# SIMPLE MANGO SORBET

## INGREDIENTS

Serves 4
Preparation time 5 minutes
Freezer time 2 hours

2 large, ripe Fairtrade mangoes
1 tbsp liquid glucose
Sprigs of fresh mint or lemon balm

## METHOD

**Peel** the mangoes. Catch and keep any juice on your chopping board. Cut the mango flesh in to chunks.

**Place** all the mango in a polythene container and freeze for 2 hours. (Do not leave for longer, or the fruit will become too hard to chop with a blending machine.)

**Remove** from the freezer, prise the pieces apart, and place them in a food processor along with the reserved juice. Add the liquid glucose and blend until smooth.

**Return** the purée to the container and refreeze. (Allow a minimum of 30 minutes. Longer is fine.)

**Transfer** to a serving dish or to individual bowls, using an ice-cream scoop to serve in rounded shapes.

**Decorate** with the sprigs of mint or lemon balm and serve.

# CLEANSING, REFRESHING, IMPOSSIBLE TO RESIST

**Anne-Marie O'Farrell** from Dublin

# CHOCOLATE AND GINGER COOKIES

## INGREDIENTS

Makes about 30 cookies
Preparation time 5 minutes
Cooking time 15–18 minutes
in batches

3 tsp Fairtrade ground ginger
275g (10oz) self-raising flour

225g (8oz) organic butter, softened
150g (5½oz) Fairtrade Demerara sugar
(plus a little extra for sprinkling)
100g (3½oz) Fairtrade organic dark
chocolate (Green & Black's Maya Gold
is excellent), broken into smallish
chunks

## METHOD

**Preheat** the oven to 150°C/300°F/Gas Mark 2. Grease two baking trays with some of the butter and set them aside.

**Sift** the ground ginger with the flour. Then mix them together with all of the other ingredients until you get a stiffish dough.

**Using** your hands, roll the dough into about 30 walnut-sized balls. Arrange them, spaced well apart, on the baking trays.

**Squash** each ball lightly with the back of a fork, leaving indentations.

**Sprinkle** a little more Demerara sugar onto each cookie for extra crunch.

**Place** in the oven for approximately 10–12 minutes until lightly golden.

**Remove** from the oven and leave for a few minutes to harden before cooling on a wire rack. Store in an airtight container.

*Tip* You could add a little chopped stem ginger for extra kick.

**Mr R Lewis** from Exeter

# IRISH TEACAKE

## INGREDIENTS

Serves 10
Preparation time 20 minutes plus
overnight soaking
Cooking time 45–50 minutes

450g (1lb) Fairtrade dried mixed fruit
(your choice of a mixture of apricots,
chopped mangoes, sultanas, raisins)
100ml (3½fl oz) strong cold Fairtrade tea

225g (8oz) Fairtrade Demerara sugar
A little butter for greasing
115g (4oz) walnuts or Fairtrade brazil
nuts, chopped
115g (4oz) glacé cherries, rinsed, dried,
and chopped into quarters
1 large egg, beaten together with 2 tbsp
milk

## METHOD

**Prepare** the fruit by soaking it in the tea and sugar and leaving it overnight.

**The** next day simply stir in all the remaining ingredients.

**Preheat** the oven to 180°C/350°F/Gas Mark 4. Thoroughly grease an 18 x 22cm (7 x 9in) shallow cake tin.

**Spread** the mixture into the tin and place in the centre of the oven. Bake for 45–50 minutes.

**Turn** the loaf out straightaway.

**Serve** warm spread with butter.

# PACKED WITH YOUR OWN CHOICE FAIRTRADE FRUIT

**Jennifer Thompson** from Keynsham Fairtrade Group, Downend, Bristol

# WHOLEMEAL FRUITCAKE

HIGHLY COMMENDED

## INGREDIENTS

Serves approximately 12
Preparation time 30 minutes
Cooking time 1 hour

115g (4oz) each dried cherries, Fairtrade stoned dried dates, and Fairtrade dried apricots, all chopped

115g (4oz) mixed peel plus 225g (8oz) Fairtrade sultanas, or 115g (4oz) Fairtrade sultanas and 115g (4oz) Fairtrade raisins, or 340g (12oz) Fairtrade mixed dried fruit

140g (5oz) butter

275ml (½ pint plus 2 tbsp) milk

3 level tbsp each Fairtrade soft brown sugar and Fairtrade white sugar

225g (8oz) wholemeal self-raising flour

½ tsp each Fairtrade mace, Fairtrade nutmeg, and Fairtrade cinnamon, and a little Fairtrade ground ginger

2 large eggs, beaten

40g (1½ oz) walnuts or Fairtrade cashew nuts, chopped (optional)

1 level tbsp Fairtrade Demerara sugar

### Optional topping

3 tbsp Fairtrade apricot or Fairtrade strawberry jam or Fairtrade marmalade

1 tbsp brandy

40g (1½ oz) walnut halves, Fairtrade brazil nuts, Fairtrade cashew nuts, or others, to taste, toasted

90g (3oz) glacé cherries

## METHOD

**Place** all the dried fruit, butter, milk, and brown and white sugars in a medium saucepan. Heat gently, then simmer for 5 minutes, stirring occasionally.

**Remove** from the heat and allow to cool. Preheat the oven to 160°C/325°F/Gas Mark 3. Line a 20cm (8in) round cake tin with parchment paper.

**Mix** the flour and spices together in a bowl. Gradually mix this into the fruit mixture, along with the eggs and nuts, if using. Place the mixture in the tin. Level off the top and sprinkle with the Demerara sugar. Bake for 30 minutes, then cover the top of the cake and bake for a further half hour.

**For** the optional topping, place the jam, or marmalade, and brandy in a pan and heat gently, stirring. Spread half the mixture over the finished cake

**Arrange** the toasted nuts and the glacé cherries on the cake. Glaze it all over with the remainder of the jam and brandy mixture.

**Judges' note** This cake looks absolutely beautiful and it tastes every bit as good as it looks.

**Cath Greenlees** Longton, Preston

# HUXLEY HEDGEHOG BISCUITS

## INGREDIENTS

Makes about 20
Preparation time 40 minutes
Cooking time 10-15 minutes

50g (1¾ oz) Fairtrade cashew nuts, chopped very small

200g (7oz) plain flour, plus extra if needed

150g (5½oz) butter or soft margarine

1 large egg

150g (5½oz) Fairtrade golden granulated sugar

1 tsp baking powder

100g (3½oz) Fairtrade mixed dried fruit (or any of your choice), chopped very small

200g (7oz) Fairtrade dark chocolate, 50g (1¾ oz) of it chopped and set aside

100g (3½oz) Fairtrade dried mango

## METHOD

**Preheat** the oven to 190°C/375°F/Gas Mark 5. Spread the chopped nuts on a baking sheet and toast for 4-5 minutes until lightly golden.

**Place** the flour, butter or margarine, egg, sugar, baking powder, mixed dried fruit, and toasted nuts into a roomy bowl and mix together to form a large ball. If it is too wet, mix more flour into the mixture.

**Roll** small balls out of this mixture, inserting a small piece of chocolate into each ball, and place on a greased baking sheet. Pinch one end to create a teardrop shape. (See tip.)

**Place** in the hot oven for 10-15 minutes or until the biscuits are light brown and firm to the touch.

**Leave** to cool on a wire rack once they have cooked.

**Melt** the remaining chocolate in a bowl over a pan of simmering water and remove from the heat.

**Cut** the dried mango into small strips.

**Dip** the fat end of each biscuit into the melted chocolate, or coat each end with chocolate using a spoon. Place on a wire rack.

**Position** the strips of mango on the chocolate to make the hedgehog's spikes. Use the chopped chocolate, mango, or dried fruit for the eyes of the hedgehog.

*Tip* You can chill the biscuits briefly before baking them to help them hold their shape in the oven.

**Mrs E Penhearow** from Bicester, Oxon

# FRUITY APPLE CAKE

## INGREDIENTS

Serves 16
Preparation time 20 minutes
Cooking time 1 hour

450g (1lb) Fairtrade eating apples, cut into 1cm (½in) chunks
175g (6oz) butter or hard margarine, plus a little extra for greasing
175g (6oz) Fairtrade granulated sugar

2 large eggs
200g (7oz) self-raising flour
1 tsp bicarbonate of soda
1 tsp Fairtrade mixed spice
50g (1¾oz) crystallized ginger, chopped
250g (9oz) Fairtrade mixed dried fruit, chopped
100g (3½oz) walnuts, chopped

## METHOD

**Simmer** the chopped apples in just enough water to cover until soft. Drain off the excess water.

**Preheat** the oven to 160°C/325°F/Gas Mark 3. Grease a 25cm (10in) round cake tin and set aside. Cream together the butter or margarine, sugar, and eggs. Add the flour, bicarbonate of soda, and mixed spice.

**Fold** in the cooked apples, the crystallized ginger, the dried fruit, and the walnuts.

**Spoon** into a greased 25cm (10in) round cake tin.

**Place** in the oven and bake for 1 hour.

**Cool** for 10 minutes before removing from tin.

**John Davidson** from Bradford, West Yorkshire

CHAPTER THREE

LIGHT BITES

# RICE AND CORN CAKES WITH SPICY PRAWNS

## INGREDIENTS

Serves 4
Preparation time 45 minutes
Cooking time 20-30 minutes

### For the corn cakes
125g (4½oz) Fairtrade rice
1 tsp Fairtrade ground turmeric
330g (11½oz) can sweetcorn, drained
pinch of chilli powder
2 large eggs, beaten
1 tbsp fresh coriander, chopped

Salt and Fairtrade black pepper
3 tbsp olive oil

### For the prawns
2cm (¾in) piece fresh root ginger, finely grated
1 large clove garlic, peeled and sliced
2-3 red chillies, deseeded and finely chopped
16 raw tiger prawns, peeled and tail on
1 large Fairtrade lemon

## METHOD

**Cook** the rice according to the pack instructions but adding in the turmeric. Drain and cool.

**Mix** the cooled rice with the sweetcorn, chilli powder, eggs, and chopped coriander in a large bowl. Season well with salt and black pepper. Divide the mixture into eight cakes.

**Heat** 2 tbsp of the olive oil in a large frying pan. Cooking in two batches, add four cakes to the frying pan and cook on a medium heat for 3-4 minutes until set and golden brown. Then turn and continue to cook until the other side is golden.

**Place** on a plate with kitchen paper to drain, and keep warm while you cook the prawns.

**Heat** the remaining oil in a large frying pan or wok. Add the ginger, garlic, and chillies, and cook for a minute until fragrant.

**Add** the prawns and cook, stirring them for 3-4 minutes until they turn pink.

**Squeeze** the juice from the lemon over the prawns and cook for another minute. Season them well and serve with the rice cakes.

*Tip* This is delicious served on a bed of fresh rocket with the prawns.

**Rosie Green** from Marist Convent School, Sunninghill, Berkshire

# SECRET SOUP

## INGREDIENTS

Serves 4
Preparation time 5 minutes
Cooking time 35 minutes

25g (1oz) butter
1 large onion, chopped
1 small clove garlic, finely chopped
1 tbsp curry powder

1 small Fairtrade banana, peeled and
  roughly chopped
2 large potatoes, peeled and roughly
  chopped
1 litre (1¾ pints) chicken stock
Salt and Fairtrade black pepper
60ml (2oz) single cream
1 good bunch fresh coriander, chopped

## METHOD

**Place** the butter in a large saucepan over a medium heat. Add the onion and garlic and cook in the butter for about 5 minutes until soft.

**Sprinkle** in the curry powder and cook for 1 minute.

**Add** the banana and potatoes, stir, and then pour in the stock.

**Bring** to a boil and simmer for approximately 30 minutes. Remove from the heat and allow to cool.

**Blend** to a smooth texture with a hand-held blender.

**Gently** reheat, but do not boil.

**Check** for seasoning, adding salt and pepper to taste.

**Serve** with a swirl of single cream and a good heaped tablespoon of fresh coriander in each bowl.

*Tip* This soup is called 'Secret' because guests will have fun trying to guess the secret ingredient – banana!

**Mrs G M Jackson** from Belfast

# ORIGINAL SUPERFOODS SALAD

## Allegra McEvedy

This is one of only two dishes that has been on the Leon menu since we first opened our doors in London's Carnaby Street over three years ago. Something magic happens when these ingredients get together, and even after all this time I still find myself craving it on a scarily frequent basis! Coupled with using Fairtrade ingredients, and being absolutely delicious, of course, it really does tick all of our boxes.

## INGREDIENTS

Serves 2
Preparation time 15 minutes;
Cooking time 15–20 minutes

30g (1oz) Fairtrade quinoa

200g (7oz) broccoli, cut into bite-sized florets

120g (4oz) peas, fresh or frozen

100g (3½oz) cucumber, cut into slim batons

100g (3½oz) good-quality feta cheese, crumbled

20g (¾oz) alfalfa

20g (¾oz) toasted seeds (we use Fairtrade sesame seeds, and sunflower, flax, and pumpkin seeds)

50g (1¾oz) Fairtrade avocado, cut into bite-sized chunks

Small handful flat-leaf parsley, roughly chopped

Small handful mint, roughly chopped

2 dessertspoons juice of a Fairtrade lemon

4 dessertspoons extra virgin olive oil

Salt and Fairtrade black pepper

## METHOD

**Put** the quinoa in a small pan. Cover with cold water plus about an inch, then let it gently simmer until the water's gone – about 15 minutes. Spread it on a tray to cool to room temperature.

**Pour** an inch of hot water into a saucepan with a pinch of salt and cover it. Once boiling, drop in the broccoli and peas and put the lid back on. Drain after three minutes and run the veg under cold water to take all the heat out and keep them crisp and green.

**Build** your salad in layers now, either individually or on a mains plate to share – this is more of a flat salad than a big-bowl affair. Start with the first ingredient on the list and end up with the chopped herbs.

**Lightly** whisk the lemon juice and oil together with some seasoning, but only dress the salad just before you eat it.

# CHICKEN, APRICOT, AND ALMOND RICE

## INGREDIENTS

Serves 4-6
Preparation time 10 minutes plus
soaking time
Cooking time 25-30 minutes

350g (12oz) Fairtrade basmati rice
½ tsp Fairtrade ground turmeric
12 Fairtrade dried apricots

Zest and juice of 1 Fairtrade orange
50g (1¾oz) flaked almonds
1 tbsp olive oil
1 red onion, chopped
6 chicken thigh fillets, sliced
15g (½oz) fresh coriander, roughly
   chopped

## METHOD

**Cook** the rice according to the instructions on the pack, but adding the turmeric to the water. When cooked, drain and set aside to keep warm.

**Soak** the apricots in half of the orange juice for 10 minutes while the rice is cooking. Drain, then halve the apricots and set them aside.

**Toast** the almonds in a large deep frying pan for 2-3 minutes until golden. Remove and set aside.

**Heat** the oil in the same pan and cook the onion over a low heat for 4-5 minutes until soft. Stir in the chicken, raise the heat, and fry for 6-8 minutes until thoroughly cooked.

**Add** the cooked rice along with the apricots, and stir through. Season well.

**Pour** in the remaining orange juice, sprinkle with almonds and herbs, and serve.

*Tip* If you prefer, you can use chopped fresh flat-leaf parsley or mint instead of chopped coriander for this dish, and maybe sprinkle over some Fairtrade ground cinnamon or a drizzle of Fairtrade honey to serve. This is a great, quick supper dish, and perfect for using up cooked chicken.

# NUTRITIOUS, QUICK, AND DEAD EASY TO PREPARE

**Jools Bryson** from Glasgow

# MALAWIAN PEANUT FUTALI

## INGREDIENTS

Serves 4–6
Preparation time 5–10 minutes;
Cooking time approximately 15 minutes

4 medium-sized sweet potatoes or cassava or half a pumpkin, washed and peeled and cut into pieces

60g (2oz) peanut flour
Pinch of salt
A handful of Fairtrade peanuts, chopped, to garnish

## METHOD

**Bring** a large saucepan of water to the boil. Add the sweet potatoes (or cassava or pumpkin) pieces and cook until almost tender.

**Drain** the water off once they are cooked.

**Add** the peanut flour and salt, and mash everything together.

**Stir** continuously, and continue cooking for a further few minutes until the mixture is almost dry. Garnish with Fairtrade peanuts.

**Serve** immediately.

*Tip* If you have difficulty getting hold of peanut flour, try an Asian or African supermarket.

# GREEN TEA CHICKEN WITH LEMON RICE

## INGREDIENTS

Serves 4
Preparation time 10 minutes
Cooking time 15 minutes

4 Fairtrade green tea bags
4 Fairtrade lemons, zest and juice
2 tbsp Fairtrade runny honey

4 chicken breasts, skinless and boneless
200g (7oz) Fairtrade basmati rice, rinsed
3 tbsp olive oil
Half of a 15g (½oz) pack chives, chopped
Salt and Fairtrade black pepper

## METHOD

**Place** the green tea, lemon zest, and honey in a large dish. Pour over 200ml (7fl oz) of hot water.

**Add** the chicken once the mixture has cooled, and chill overnight, covered, in the fridge.

**Place** the rice in a pan when you are ready to make the chicken dish. Cook the rice according to the instructions on the pack and keep it warm.

**Drain** the chicken from the marinade while the rice is cooking. Discard the marinade. Pat the chicken dry and season it well.

**Heat** a griddle pan with 1 tbsp of the oil and cook the chicken breasts for 4–5 minutes on each side until thoroughly cooked.

**Stir** the lemon juice, the 2 remaining tbsp of olive oil and the chives into the rice and season well. Serve straight away with the grilled chicken on the side.

*Tip* This is delicious served with asparagus or sprouting broccoli.

# A MARINATED CHICKEN DISH FOR ANY SEASON

**Andrew Dobson** from Addiscombe, Croydon

# PIQUANT PRAWN AND PINEAPPLE PILAF

## INGREDIENTS

Serves 4
Preparation time 20 minutes
Cooking time 15 minutes

300g (10 oz) Fairtrade quinoa, rinsed
2 tbsp olive oil
1 red onion, finely chopped
2 Fairtrade red peppers, deseeded, and chopped
1 small Fairtrade pineapple, peeled, cored, and diced
1 medium Fairtrade mango, peeled, stone removed, and diced
1 large red chilli, deseeded and finely chopped
1 tsp Fairtrade ground ginger
400g (14oz) raw king prawns, peeled
1 Fairtrade lemon, zest and juice
15g (½oz) bunch fresh coriander, chopped

## METHOD

**Cook** the quinoa according to the pack instructions and set aside.

**Heat** the oil meanwhile in a large frying pan or wok.

**Add** the onion and pepper and cook for 8–10 minutes until softened.

**Stir** in the pineapple, mango, chilli, and ginger, and cook for 2 minutes

**Add** the prawns and cook for 2–3 minutes, stirring until they have turned pink and are cooked.

**Add** the lemon zest and juice. Gently fold in the quinoa and most of the coriander.

**Divide** between 4 serving plates and garnish with remaining coriander.

**Mrs Carole Jones** from Colsterworth, Lincolnshire

# SALMON KOULIBIACA

## Oz Clarke

My father was a doctor heavily involved in health projects throughout the third world and, from childhood, I have been deeply aware of the inequalities many people endure around the world, so the Fairtrade movement particularly resonates with me. I have visited wine producers in South Africa, Chile, and Argentina supplying the Fairtrade market. Fairtrade is about self-help, with people on the ground organizing themselves. It is not about sitting around waiting for hand-outs. It is about offering a hand up.

## INGREDIENTS

Serves 4
Preparation time 45 minutes
Cooking time 25-30 minutes

50g (1¾oz) Fairtrade rice
1 Fairtrade lemon
450g (1lb) piece salmon fillet
100ml (3½fl oz) Fairtrade white wine
A knob of butter
250g (9oz) mushrooms, sliced

1 small onion, finely sliced
15 Fairtrade grapes, halved
25g (1oz) Fairtrade raisins
Handful flaked almonds
Salt and freshly ground Fairtrade black pepper
375g (13oz) pack ready-made puff pastry
1 large egg, beaten

## METHOD

**Preheat** the oven to 200°C/400°F/Gas Mark 6. Cook the rice for 18 minutes, drain it, allow it to cool. Grate half of the lemon zest finely and mix with the rice. Pare off the remaining zest in wide strips. Cut the lemon in half and squeeze out the juice.

**Poach** the salmon in water with a glass of wine, strips of lemon zest, and the juice until cooked through – about 15 minutes. Lift the fish out and let it cool for 5 minutes or so.

**Melt** the butter in a pan and add the sliced mushrooms and onion and fry gently for 5 minutes. Then leave to cool slightly. Flake the salmon and mix with the rice in a bowl. Add the grapes, raisins, and almonds, and season.

**Spread** the salmon mix over the centre of the rolled-out puff pastry leaving plenty of room round the outside. Layer the mushroom and onion mixture on top of the salmon.

**Fold** the ends and sides of the pastry up and over the filling and pinch the edges to seal. Put the pastry parcel, seam sides down, on a greased baking tray. Brush the beaten egg over the outside of the pastry. Prick with a fork. Cook for 25-30 minutes or until the pastry is risen and golden.

# WINTER SALAD

## INGREDIENTS

Serves 4
Preparation time 20 minutes
Cooking time 20 minutes

250g (9oz) Fairtrade quinoa
2 tsp Fairtrade dried oregano
40g (1½oz) sunflower seeds, toasted
2 medium-sized Fairtrade avocados,
    peeled, stone removed, and sliced into
    2cm (¾in) dice

Half a small red onion, finely sliced
2 sticks celery, finely sliced
2 large Fairtrade oranges
2 bunches watercress, rinsed and dried
2 tbsp olive oil

## METHOD

**Place** the quinoa and oregano into a non-stick pan and cover with 500ml (1 pint) boiling water. Bring to the boil and immediately turn down the heat to its lowest setting. Meanwhile, preheat the grill and spread the sunflower seeds on to a grill pan. Gently toast the seeds until they turn golden brown but keep an eye on them so they don't burn. When they are finished set them aside.

**When** all the liquid in the quinoa has been absorbed (after 15–20 minutes), turn off the heat and leave the quinoa to cool in the pan.

**Place** the diced avocado in a salad bowl with the red onion and celery.

**Peel** and segment the oranges, reserving any escaped juice in another bowl, and add the orange segments to the avocado mixture.

**Discard** any large stalks of watercress, keeping the leaves. Add all the leaves and smaller stalks to the other fresh ingredients.

**Add** the olive oil to the reserved orange juice and whisk to make the dressing. Pour this over the salad ingredients. Top with the toasted sunflower seeds and toss well.

**Stir** the quinoa to separate the grains, and combine it with the rest of the salad ingredients. Divide the mixture between four serving dishes.

*Tip* On its own this salad makes a substantial supper dish but it is also a great accompaniment to grilled fish, especially mackerel, or you could serve it with soft goat cheese coated with peppercorns.

**Joanna Fox** from Leeds

# PRAWN AND MANGO CEVICHE

## Antony Worrall Thompson

Choosing Fairtrade ingredients means that together we are helping to open up more opportunities for producers like the mango farmers in Burkina Faso, one of the poorest countries in the world, for whom Fairtrade has brought a route out of poverty. I use their mangoes in this delicious recipe and I find that knowing a little more about the people who grew the mangoes makes them taste all the sweeter. And as there is now such a wide variety of different Fairtrade certified products available, there is really no reason for us all not to switch to using more Fairtrade foods.

## INGREDIENTS

Serves 4
Preparation time 15-20 minutes
Cooking time 25–30 minutes

12 raw peeled prawns, diced
2 tbsp coriander leaf, whole
1 tbsp shredded mint
1 Fairtrade avocado, peeled, stoned, and diced
1 Fairtrade mango, peeled, stoned, and diced

3 spring onions, sliced
1 red chilli, deseeded and thinly sliced
½ cucumber, peeled, seeded, and diced

### Dressing
3 tbsp Fairtrade lime juice
1½ tbsp Thai fish sauce
1 tbsp caster sugar
3 tbsp thick coconut milk

## METHOD

**Combine** the prawns with the dressing and allow them to marinate for 20 minutes.

**Combine** the remaining salad ingredients with the prawns.

**Serve** in a Martini glass or on baby gem salad leaves.

*Tip* You can garnish this recipe with chopped coriander.

# TROPICAL CHICKEN SALAD

## INGREDIENTS

Serves 4
Preparation time 10 minutes
Cooking time 45 minutes

4 chicken breasts, skinless and boneless, and cut in to strips
6 tbsp desiccated coconut
4 tsp Fairtrade ground ginger
3 tsp Fairtrade ground cinnamon
1 tsp Fairtrade ground nutmeg

½ tsp ground cloves, or freshly grind Fairtrade whole cloves
2 large Fairtrade lemons, zest and juice
2 large Fairtrade avocados, peeled, stone removed, and sliced
90g (3oz) wild rocket
1 large Fairtrade mango, peeled, stone removed, and diced
2 tbsp olive oil
2–4 tbsp Fairtrade runny honey, to taste

## METHOD

**Rinse** the chicken. Pat it dry on kitchen paper.

**Heat** the coconut in a non-stick frying pan and cook for 2–3 minutes until lightly toasted. Allow to cool.

**Place** the toasted coconut, spices, and lemon zest in a large plastic food bag and mix well.

**Add** the chicken and it season well. Seal the bag and shake it until the chicken is coated in the mixture.

**Cover** the avocado in half of the lemon juice, and place it in a serving bowl with the rocket and diced mango. Set aside.

**Heat** the oil in a large frying pan or wok until very hot. Add the spice-coated chicken and cook for 3–4 minutes, stirring constantly.

**Drizzle** over the honey and cook for another 2–3 minutes until the chicken is thoroughly done. Squeeze over the remaining lemon juice.

**Stir** the chicken into the salad ingredients and serve immediately.

*Tip* Accompany this deliciously different dish with new potatoes. You can also use young-leaf spinach instead of rocket if you prefer.

**Judges' note:** This is a fresh and invigorating recipe. You may find that it is already sweet enough without the honey.

**Mrs S Marsland** from Wotton under Edge, Gloucestershire

# KEDGEREE

## Hugh Fearnley-Whittingstall

Good food always has a good story – it has character because it's produced by people with names. Fairtrade products give us a little taste of those stories, and a feeling of connection with the lives of those producers. It always feels good to be cooking with ingredients produced by people who are rewarded and looked after for the work they do.

## INGREDIENTS

Serves 4
Preparation time 15 minutes
Cooking time 25–30 minutes

300ml (10fl oz) whole milk
1 bay leaf
400g (14oz) smoked pollack or haddock
1 tbsp olive oil
a good knob of butter
1 large onion, peeled and finely sliced from tip to root
2 tsp mild curry powder

175g (6oz) Fairtrade basmati rice, rinsed in cold water a few times and drained
4 large free-range eggs, hard boiled and peeled
2 tbsp chopped coriander
another knob of butter
1 tbsp finely chopped lovage (optional garnish)
Fairtrade lemon wedges
good twist of Fairtrade trade black pepper

## METHOD

**Put** the milk and 300ml (10fl oz) water in a shallow pan with the bay leaf and fish. Cover and bring to a gentle simmer. By the time the liquid is simmering, the fish should be cooked through. If not, turn the fillet over in the hot liquid and leave it, off the heat, for 2–3 minutes to finish cooking.

**Remove** the fish and set aside. Remove the bay leaf and reserve the poaching liquid. When it's cool enough to handle, break the poached fish into flakes, discarding the skin and picking out any bones.

**Heat** the olive oil and butter a large saucepan. Add the onion and cook gently for 8–10 minutes. Stir in the curry powder, then the rice. Add 300ml (10fl oz) of the poaching liquid. Bring to the boil and then cover the pan. Turn the heat down to bare minimum and cook for 15 minutes. Remove from the heat and fluff up the rice with a fork. Set aside with the lid back on until you're ready to assemble the dish.

**Fold** the smoked fish flakes into the rice, along with half the coarsely chopped coriander and the second knob of butter. Cut the hard-boiled eggs in half – with luck they'll still be just a bit soft in the middle.

**Spoon** the spicy, fishy rice into four warmed plates or wide bowls, top with two hard-boiled egg halves per person, and sprinkle with more coriander – and the lovage, if you have it. Add a wedge of lemon and a good twist of black pepper and serve.

# SUMMER PRAWN AND MANGO NOODLE SALAD

## INGREDIENTS

Serves 4
Preparation time 20-25 minutes
Cooking time 5 minutes

**Dressing**
1 red chilli, finely chopped
2 tbsp Fairtrade clear honey
2 tbsp Thai fish sauce
1 tbsp mild olive oil

Juice of 1 Fairtrade lime
250g (9oz) dry weight medium egg
   noodles (4 sheets)
2 medium Fairtrade mangoes, peeled,
   stone removed, and flesh sliced in to
   thin strips
300g (10oz) cooked tiger prawns
A small bunch fresh coriander,
   roughly chopped

## METHOD

**Make** the dressing first by combining the chilli, honey, Thai fish sauce, olive oil, and lime juice, stirring well.

**Cook** the noodles according to the packet instructions. When they are ready, rinse them immediately in cold water to cool them off and stop them from continuing to cook.

**Place** the noodles in a large bowl, pour in the dressing, and mix well. Divide the dressed noodles between four individual serving bowls and top with equal amounts of the sliced mango, cooked prawns, and chopped coriander.

**Mix** each serving of salad together in its own bowl to distribute the ingredients evenly. (This is far easier than trying to dish the salad out from one large bowl containing all of the ingredients.)

*Tip* This dish keeps well in the refrigerator so you can make it earlier in the day. Make sure you don't skip the stage of cooling the noodles thoroughly, and do keep the coriander back until the last minute.

**Sophie Clarke** from Kidlington, Oxon

# JAPANESE-STYLE DUCK BREASTS WITH AROMATIC RICE

## INGREDIENTS

Serves 2 generously
Preparation time 10 minutes
Cooking time 45 minutes

125g (4½oz) Fairtrade basmati rice
1 Fairtrade cinnamon stick
1 star anise
1 tsp coriander seeds, crushed
30g (1oz) Fairtrade cashew nuts
2 tbsp red miso paste
Chilli oil to taste
1 tsp soy sauce

1 tsp mirin
5mm (¼in) fresh root ginger, finely
   chopped or grated
1 tsp seven-taste powder (use less if
   preferred)
2 duck breasts, skin scored with a knife
15g (½oz) fresh coriander, roughly
   chopped, reserving some for serving
4 spring onions, finely sliced
1 Fairtrade red pepper, cut into thin strips

## METHOD

**Preheat** oven to 160°C/325°F/Gas Mark 3. Place the rice in a saucepan of boiling water with the cinnamon, star anise, and coriander seeds. Reduce the heat, cover and cook for 10–12 minutes until tender. Season and keep warm.

**Dry-fry** the cashew nuts meanwhile in a frying pan for 2–3 minutes until lightly toasted and set aside. Mix the miso with the chilli, soy, mirin, ginger, and seven-taste powder, and set aside.

**Heat** a frying pan, add the duck breasts, skin-side down, and cook 3–5 minutes. Reserve the duck fat. Transfer the duck to a roasting dish skin-side up. Cover in half of the miso paste and cook in the oven for 10–15 minutes or until slightly pink inside. Remove and allow to rest for 5 minutes.

**Heat** a frying pan with a little of the reserved duck fat and fry the spring onion and pepper for 3–4 minutes until tender. Stir in the remaining miso paste. Remove from the heat and keep warm.

**Stir** the cashews and a dash of chilli oil into the rice, removing the star anise and cinnamon. Season well and serve with the duck and fried peppers and spring onions. Serve sprinkled with fresh coriander.

*Tip* Slice the duck breasts and serve on the aromatic rice. Look for seven-taste powder in Asian supermarkets.

**Judges' note** This dish has a wonderfully aromatic flavour.

**Alex Prichard** from Leeds

# CARIBBEAN BANANA SALAD

## INGREDIENTS

Serves 4
 Preparation time 15 minutes
 Cooking time 15-20 minutes

4 cloves garlic, crushed

60g (2oz) sliced pimiento-stuffed green olives

2 small red onions, thinly sliced

1 bay leaf

120ml (4fl oz) olive oil

120ml (4fl oz) white wine vinegar

Juice of one Fairtrade lime

Salt and Fairtrade black pepper to taste

1kg (2¼lb) very green, underripe Fairtrade bananas

## METHOD

**Combine** garlic, olives, onion, bay leaf, olive oil, vinegar, lime juice, salt, and pepper in a large bowl and set aside.

**Bring** a large pot of water of water to the boil. Meanwhile, cut the ends from the green bananas and slit peel lengthways; keep peel on.

**Boil** the bananas for a few minutes until they are soft, yet still firm. Drain bananas and place in a pan of icy water for approximately 5 minutes or until they are completely cold.

**Peel** bananas and cut into 2.5cm (1in) rounds. Add banana rounds to the bowl of garlic and onion mixture and toss to coat well. Sprinkle with the sliced red onion.

*Tip* For a more substantial salad, serve on plates lined with chopped lettuce and add tomato, Fairtrade avocado, carrot sticks, a red Fairtrade pepper cut into strips, and some broccoli florets. This dish would make a delicious accompaniment for a curry.

# MANGO, AVOCADO, AND BROWN RICE SALAD

## INGREDIENTS

Serves 3–4
Preparation time 15 minutes;
Cooking time 35 minutes

175g (6oz) Fairtrade brown basmati rice

2 Fairtrade mangoes, peeled, stone removed, and cubed

1 large ripe Fairtrade avocado, peeled, stone removed, and cubed

Half red chilli, deseeded and finely chopped

10g (⅓oz) fresh mint, roughly torn

10g (⅓oz) fresh basil, roughly torn

10g (⅓oz) fresh coriander, roughly chopped

Juice of 2 Fairtrade limes, plus grated zest of 1 Fairtrade lime

1 tablespoon olive oil

Freshly ground Fairtrade black pepper

## METHOD

**Cook** the rice in boiling water in a medium-sized pan for 35 minutes, or for the time stated on the packet, until tender. Once cooked, drain well and allow to cool.

**Place** the mango and avocado cubes, chilli, fresh herbs, lime juice and zest, and olive oil in a large bowl and season.

**Mix** together and combine with the rice when ready.

# LOTS OF DELICIOUS LIME FLAVOUR. (AND SO EASY!)

**Steven Furnival** from Market Harborough, Leicestershire

# FJORD AND FOREST SUMMER SALAD

## Natasha Kaplinsky

Cooking for me has always been more of a chore than a pleasure, so quick and easy recipes are always a winner. Having relatively recently married, I do (occasionally) feel duty bound to provide some sustenance at the end of the day. I don't eat meat, so fresh produce and plenty of fish feature quite highly. And since my husband is half Norwegian, I have tried to incorporate some traditional 'Viking' favourites, from fjord and forest. The great thing about this recipe is that it incorporates several Fairtrade ingredients and tastes all the better for knowing the farmers are being paid a better price.

## INGREDIENTS

Serves 2
Preparation time 20 minutes

Small handful Fairtrade cashew nuts, gently roasted

Small handful pine nuts

1 Fairtrade red pepper, cored, deseeded and sliced thinly

100g (3½oz) mixed salad leaves

100g (3½oz) rocket

1 handful fresh coriander, roughly chopped

250g (9oz) cooked Norwegian prawns, peeled and chopped, leaving a few whole for decoration

1 Fairtrade avocado, peeled, stone removed, and diced

### Dressing:

3 tbsp Extra virgin olive oil

Small handful of crushed wild mountain or small English strawberries

1 tsp of Fairtrade honey

Squeeze of Fairtrade lemon

1 tbsp cider vinegar

## METHOD

**Toss** together the nuts, red pepper, salad leaves, chopped coriander, and chopped prawns in a large bowl and set aside.

**Place** all the dressing ingredients in a large jar with a securely fitting lid. Place the lid on the jar and shake the contents to blend.

**Pour** the dressing over the salad and toss until coated.

**Sprinkle** the salad with the diced avocado, decorate with the whole prawns, and serve.

# TILAPIA FISH AND RICE WITH GREEN BEANS

## Adjoa Andoh

I want to be sure that the farmers who produce the goods I buy are getting a fair price for their products and will benefit directly from my purchases. Being the daughter of a Ghanaian father, I know how much small producers and co-operatives in Ghana rely on the access Fairtrade helps provide to overseas markets and I want to contribute.

## INGREDIENTS

Serves 4
Preparation time 40 minutes
Cooking time 40 minutes

4 medium-sized fillets of tilapia fish
Juice of three Fairtrade lemons
4 tbsp Fairtrade brazil nut oil
1 hot chilli pepper, sliced
8 sprigs fresh rosemary

Freshly ground Fairtrade black pepper
250g (9oz) Fairtrade basmati rice
2.5cm (1in) piece fresh turmeric, peeled and sliced
Pinch of freshly grated nutmeg
Knob of butter
250g (9oz) green beans

## METHOD

**Preheat** the oven to 200°C/400°F/Gas Mark 6. Lay each tilapia fillet in a large piece of foil. Pour the juice of half a lemon and 1 tbsp of brazil nut oil over each fillet. Place two sprigs of rosemary and a few slices of chilli on each fillet, and grind some black pepper over.

**Wrap** the fillets up in the foil and put them in a baking dish. Bake for 20–25 minutes.

**Place** the rice into a deep saucepan. Add the slices of turmeric and grated nutmeg. Add the butter and cover in boiling water plus an extra inch. Place over a medium heat, cover, and bring to the boil. Turn down to a very low simmer for about 25 minutes. When all water has been absorbed check the rice. Watch that the water does not dry out during cooking, and add more hot water as required until it is done. In the last 5 minutes of cooking, lay the beans over the rice to steam.

**Divide** the rice onto four plates, set a fish fillet on top, and place a portion of beans along the side. Grind as much fresh black pepper over as you like.

*Tip* Serve this dish with a salad of fresh Fairtrade mango and avocado, and fresh basil, all chopped and tossed together with a little Fairtrade brazil nut oil. You could also use red snapper fillets for this recipe.

# VEGETABLE, GINGER, AND PINEAPPLE CHILLI STEW

## INGREDIENTS

Serves 4
Preparation 20 minutes
Cooking time 1 hour 30 minutes

300ml (10fl oz) Fairtrade tropical or
apple juice
1½ tbsp plain flour
1 tbsp vegetable oil
1 large onion, sliced
1 heaped tsp Fairtrade ground ginger
Half a dried chilli, crumbled

800g (2lb) seasonal vegetables (carrots,
parsnips, butternut squash, celery, and
leeks work particularly well together),
cut into rough chunks
1 large onion, sliced
Half a Fairtrade fresh pineapple, roughly
chopped
200ml (7oz) hot vegetable stock
50g (1¾ oz) Fairtrade cashew nuts
Salt and Fairtrade pepper
300g (10oz) Fairtrade basmati rice

## METHOD

**Preheat** the oven to 200°C/400°F/Gas Mark 6. Add a little of the fruit juice to the flour and stir to make a smooth paste.

**Heat** the oil in a frying pan and fry the onion until tender. Stir in the ginger and chilli and cook for a further 30 seconds, then take off the heat.

**Place** the raw chopped vegetables and fresh pineapple chunks in a large casserole dish with the onions.

**Pour** in the paste, the remaining fruit juice, and the vegetable stock, and stir together.

**Cover** with a well-fitting lid and place in the oven. After 30 minutes remove it from the oven and stir in the cashew nuts. Season with salt and pepper. Stir thoroughly before returning to oven for a further 20–30 minutes or until the vegetables are tender.

**Cook** the rice according to the instructions on the packet and serve with the stew.

**Fiona Ranford** from Swindon

# PEPPERED SALMON SERVED WITH RICE AND A TANGY SAUCE

## INGREDIENTS

Serves 4
**Preparation time 15 minutes;**
**Cooking time 20-30 minutes**

300g (10 oz) Fairtrade organic brown basmati rice

4 skin-on salmon fillets, each weighing approximately 150g (5½oz)

2 tbsp olive oil

2 tsp Fairtrade peppercorns, crushed

2 Fairtrade lemons, zest and juice of 1, the other cut into wedges

2 red onions, finely chopped

3 garlic cloves, finely crushed

1 tsp Fairtrade dried dill

2 x 400g (14oz) cans chopped tomatoes

1 tsp Fairtrade granulated sugar

## METHOD

**Preheat** the oven to 180°C/350°F/Gas Mark 4. Cook the rice according to the pack instructions.

**Arrange** the salmon fillets, skin-side down on a greased ovenproof dish or baking sheet while the rice is cooking. Brush the salmon with a little oil and press with peppercorns. Squeeze over the juice of one of the lemons.

**Place** the salmon in the oven and cook for 10–15 minutes until the fish begins to flake.

**Make** the Tangy Sauce meanwhile by placing the remaining olive oil in a large pan over a medium heat. Add the onion and cook for 8–10 minutes until it has softened.

**Add** the garlic, lemon zest, and dill, and stir for 1 minute. Then add the tomatoes and sugar and simmer for 10 minutes until the sauce has slightly reduced.

**Place** a bed of rice on each plate along with a portion of Tangy Sauce. Cut the remaining lemon into wedges. Sit a salmon fillet on top of the rice and serve each one with a lemon wedge.

**Beverley Frith** from Walkley, Sheffield

CHAPTER FOUR

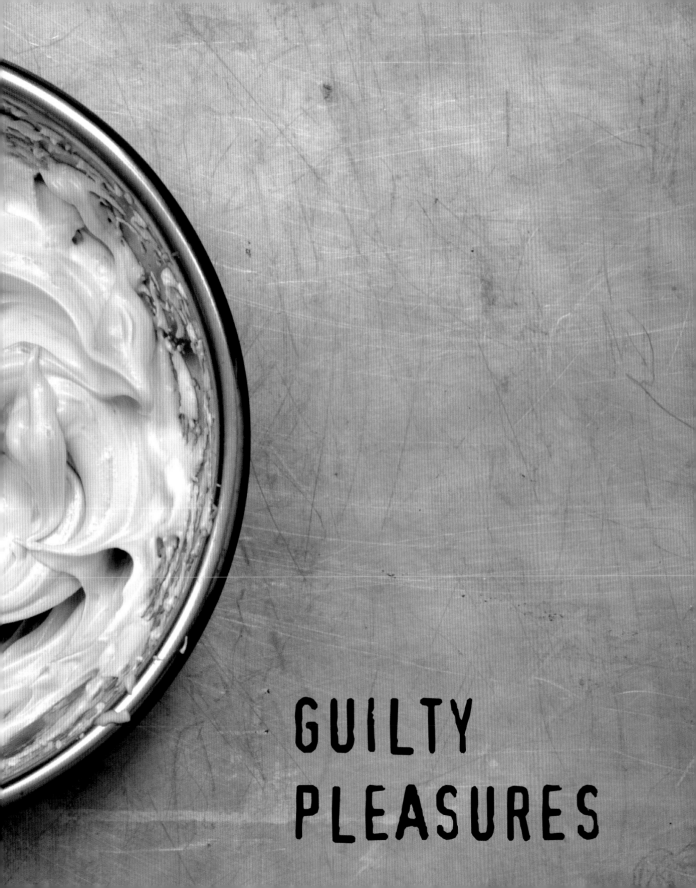

GUILTY
PLEASURES

# BUSY DAY MOCHA BANANA CAKE

## INGREDIENTS

Makes 16 slices
Preparation time 20 minutes
Cooking time 20 minutes

2 extra-ripe large Fairtrade bananas
1 tbsp Fairtrade instant coffee granules
155g (5½oz) plain flour
120g (4oz) Fairtrade white granulated
  sugar
25g (¾oz) cornflour
25g (¾oz) Fairtrade organic cocoa
2 tsp baking soda
½tsp salt

1 Fairtrade vanilla pod
1 large egg, lightly beaten
80ml (2¾fl oz) vegetable oil
1 tbsp vinegar

### Frosting
40g (1½oz) butter, softened
230g (8oz) sifted icing sugar
30g (1oz) Fairtrade organic cocoa
1 tbsp Fairtrade instant coffee granules
2 tbsp milk

## METHOD

**Mix** and bake the cake in one tin. Preheat the oven to 180°C/350°F/Gas Mark 4. Slice the bananas into a blender, and blend until smooth.

**Stir** the coffee granules into the bananas and set aside.

**Combine** the flour, sugar, cornflour, cocoa, baking soda, and salt in the middle of a 23cm (9in) square tin, and blend it well with a fork. Split the vanilla pod and scrape out the seeds.

**Make** a well in the centre of the dry ingredients. Add the banana mixture, egg, oil, vinegar, and two-thirds of the vanilla seeds. Stir until the wet ingredients are blended into the dry.

**Place** in the middle of the oven and bake for 30 minutes.

**Cool** in the tin.

**Make** the frosting by combining the butter, sugar, cocoa, and coffee. Add the milk and the remaining vanilla seeds, and beat until smooth. Spread on the cooled cake, in the pan, and cut in to slices to serve.

*Tip* Instead of using a vanilla pod, you can use 1 tsp Fairtrade vanilla extract.

**Karin Holloway** from London

# HONEY AND COCONUT COOKIES

## INGREDIENTS

Makes 12
Preparation time 20 minutes
Cooking time 10 minutes

150g (5½oz) plain flour
50g (1¾oz) Fairtrade soft brown sugar

50g (1¾ oz) caster sugar
1 large egg, beaten
2 tbsp Fairtrade honey
50g (1¾ oz) desiccated coconut
2 tbsp vegetable oil

## METHOD

**Preheat** oven to 180°C/350°F/Gas Mark 4.

**Mix** the flour and brown and white sugars in a large bowl.

**Add** the beaten egg, honey, and coconut.

**Gradually** add the oil to form a firm dough.

**Using** floured hands, roll the dough into 12 balls and arrange them on a greased baking tray.

**Flatten** each cookie with the back of a spoon and bake for approximately 10 minutes until golden brown.

**Leave** to cool on the baking tray for a few minutes before placing on a cooling rack.

# KEEP A SUPPLY OF THESE READY FOR WHEN COOKIE CRAVINGS STRIKE

**Sarah Hawtree, Emily Nicholls, and Rebecca Ward**
from Archbishop Holgate School, York

# SPICED PINEAPPLE CAKE

## INGREDIENTS

Serves 8-10
Preparation time: 20 minutes
Cooking time 50 minutes

50g (1¾oz) Fairtrade Demerara sugar
5 tbsp Fairtrade rum
1 small Fairtrade pineapple, peeled,
   cored, and sliced into rounds

225g (8oz) self-raising flour
1½ tsp baking powder
1 tsp Fairtrade mixed spice
1 tsp Fairtrade ground cinnamon
225g (8oz) caster sugar
3 large eggs
225g (8oz) butter or soft margarine

## METHOD

**Preheat** the oven to 180°C/350°F/Gas Mark 4. Line the base of a 19cm (7½in) square cake tin with parchment paper.

**Place** the Demerara sugar and 3 tbsp of the rum in a saucepan and bring to a boil. Reduce the heat, and simmer for 5 minutes.

**Arrange** four pineapple slices into the base of the cake tin. Pour over the rum syrup and set aside.

**Sieve** together the flour, baking powder, and spices.

**Add** the caster sugar, eggs, and butter or margarine, and beat together until thoroughly combined.

**Chop** the remaining pineapple into small pieces and fold them into the cake mixture.

**Pour** the mixture into the tin, level it with the back of a spoon, and bake for 50 minutes. Cover it with greaseproof paper after 30 minutes if it is browning too quickly.

**Pierce** a skewer into the centre of the cake. If it comes out clean the cake is done.

**Remove** the cake from the oven and place it, still in the tin, on a cooling rack. Remove the greaseproof paper from the top, if used.

**After** 10 minutes insert a skewer all over cake and pour over the remaining 2 tbsp of rum.

**Allow** to cool completely before turning out onto a presentation plate.

**Judges' note** This cake makes a lovely Sunday lunch pudding served warm with custard or whipped cream.

**Miss Samantha Park** from Maidstone, Kent

# CHOCOLATE AND CHESTNUT TERRINE

## INGREDIENTS

Serves 4-6
Preparation 30 minutes plus
overnight chilling
Half of a 250g (9oz) pack plain Rich Tea
   Fingers
1 large egg yolk

35g (1 ¼oz) Fairtrade granulated sugar
100g (3½oz) Fairtrade dark chocolate
85g (3oz) butter, softened
270g (9½oz) sweetened chestnut purée
25g (1oz) crème fraiche
2 tbsp kirsch (optional)

## METHOD

**Line** a 450g (1lb) loaf tin with a double thickness of cling film. Then line the bottom and sides of the tin with biscuits, cut to fit, and set aside. Beat the egg yolk and sugar together until they are a pale creamy colour and thick texture.

**Gently** melt the chocolate in a bowl over a pan of simmering water or in a microwave, then remove from the heat. Pour into the egg mixture and stir to combine. In another bowl whisk the butter until it is very soft, then beat the chocolate mixture into the butter.

**Add** the chestnut purée little by little, then the crème fraîche, and finally the kirsch, if using.

**Spoon** one-third of the chocolate mixture followed by a layer of biscuits into the prepared loaf tin. Repeat the layers finishing with a layer of biscuits.

**Cover** with cling film, then kitchen foil, and weigh down with some cans to help compress the terrine.

**Place** in the fridge overnight.

**After** the terrine has chilled and set, remove the weights, foil, and cling film and invert the tin. Carefully unmould the terrine from the loaf tin onto a serving plate.

*Tip* You can decorate the terrine with a dusting of icing sugar, chocolate shavings, or sprigs of fresh mint. Serve it with crème anglaise, crème fraîche, or double cream.

**Philippe Bruyer** from London

# COOKIE FEAST PIZZA

## INGREDIENTS

Serves 10
Preparation time 15 minutes
Baking time 18 minutes

75g (2½oz) organic butter, softened
75g (2½oz) Fairtrade peanut butter
225g (8oz) plain flour
100g (3½oz) Fairtrade raw cane sugar
1 medium egg, beaten

½tsp Fairtrade vanilla extract
4 tbsp Fairtrade chocolate and hazelnut
   spread
150g (5½oz) miniature marshmallows
50g (1¾oz) Fairtrade Green & Black's
   Maya Gold chocolate, roughly chopped
75g (2½oz) Fairtrade mini
   chocolate eggs

## METHOD

**Preheat** the oven to 180°C/350°F/Gas Mark 4.

**Cream** the butter and peanut butter in a bowl with an electric beater until smooth and creamy.

**Add** the flour, sugar, egg, and vanilla extract, and beat until combined.

**Press** the dough into a pizza pan or baking sheet to make a 30cm (12in) circle with a small rim.

**Place** in the oven and bake for 10 minutes until almost firm to touch.

**Remove** the cookie and cover it with the chocolate and hazelnut spread, leaving a 1cm (½in) gap around the edge.

**Sprinkle** with the marshmallows and chopped chocolate. Place the cookie back in the oven and bake for a further 5–6 minutes until the marshmallows are golden and puffy.

**Remove** the cookie pizza from the oven and sprinkle it with the mini eggs. Leave the cookie pizza to cool for 5 minutes and then serve it cut in wedges.

**Michelle Swann** from Doncaster

# EASY-MAKE TROPICAL BANANA CAKE

## INGREDIENTS

Serves 12
Preparation time 20 minutes
Cooking time 35–40 minutes

3 ripe Fairtrade bananas, mashed
115g (4oz) butter or soft low-fat
  margarine
115g (4oz) Fairtrade golden granulated
  sugar
2 large eggs

170g (6oz) organic flour (85g/3oz self-
  raising white plus 85g/3oz self-raising
  wholemeal)
3 tbsp Fairtrade Fruit Passion juice (2 tbsp
  to mix with cake mix and 1 tbsp to
  make icing)
1 tsp baking powder
Pinch of Fairtrade ground cinnamon
1 tbsp Fairtrade orange marmalade
85g (3oz) icing sugar

## METHOD

**Preheat** the oven to 180°C/350°F/Gas Mark 4. Grease an 18cm (7in) square cake tin.

**Put** all the ingredients except the icing sugar in a very large mixing bowl. (Keep back 1 tbsp of the juice.)

**Using** an electric hand-held whisk, mix the ingredients until thoroughly combined.

**Spoon** the batter into the cake tin. Bake for approximately 45 minutes until a skewer inserted into the cake comes out clean.

**Mix** the icing sugar and remaining juice in a small bowl until a runny consistency is formed. Add more sugar and juice if necessary.

**When** the cake is finished, allow it to cool and then remove it from the tin and stand it on a wire rack.

**Drizzle** the cake with the icing.

*Tip* The cooking time might be longer if you use a round tin.

**Christine Cardy** from Felixstowe, Suffolk

# GRANDMA'S CHOCOLATE CHUNK GINGER BISCUITS

## INGREDIENTS

Makes 30–35 biscuits
Preparation time 10 minutes
Cooking time 10 minutes

250g (9oz) butter or margarine
3 tbsp molasses
3 tbsp Fairtrade golden syrup

450g (1lb) self-raising flour
4 tbsp Fairtrade Demerara sugar
3 heaped tsp Fairtrade ground ginger
½ tsp Fairtrade ground cinnamon
100g (3½oz) Fairtrade chocolate, broken
  into fairly large chunks

## METHOD

**Preheat** the oven to 180°C/350°F/Gas Mark 4. Grease a couple of baking trays.

**Melt** the butter or margarine, molasses, and syrup together in a pan over a low heat, stirring to combine.

**Mix** the dry ingredients, except the chocolate, in a bowl, then add the melted ingredients.

**Add** the chocolate and stir the mix to combine. The chocolate should melt slightly but there should be some lumps left in the mixture. (If your mixture is too dry, you can add a few drops of milk until it binds together.)

**Roll** the mixture into walnut-sized balls and arrange them on the greased baking trays.

**Bake** the biscuits in batches for 10 minutes.

*Tip* These are good without the chocolate as well. You can use 6 tbsp of golden syrup if you have difficulty finding molasses. Make sure you use walnut-sized balls of dough as these biscuits are really filling if they are any bigger.

**Holly Greenwood** from Stratford-upon-Avon

# RICH DUNDEE CAKE

## INGREDIENTS

Serves 12
Preparation time 20 minutes
Cooking time 3 hours

170g (6oz) butter
170g (6oz) Fairtrade raw cane sugar or
   dark muscovado sugar
4 medium eggs, beaten
2 tbsp black treacle
1 tsp each Fairtrade ground nutmeg,
   Fairtrade ground cinnamon,
   Fairtrade ground cloves, and Fairtrade
   mixed spices, sifted together

170g (6oz) self-raising flour
340g (12oz) currants
225g (8oz) Fairtrade sultanas
225g (8oz) Fairtrade raisins
55g (2oz) mixed peel
55g (2oz) blanched almonds for
   decoration

## METHOD

**Preheat** the oven to 150°C/300°F/Gas Mark 2. Grease and line a 20cm (8in) round tin and set it aside.

**Cream** the butter and sugar together in a large bowl.

**Add** the beaten eggs and treacle and stir to combine.

**Mix** in the spices and fold in the flour.

**Add** the fruit and mix everything well.

**Place** the mixture into the prepared tin, arrange the nuts on top, and protect with brown paper.

**Bake** for 3 hours, but test after 2½ hours with a skewer.

*Tip* You could use (850g) 1lb 14oz Fairtrade mixed dried fruit instead of the recommended mixture.

**Ursula Dove** from Bobbersmill, Nottingham

# INDULGENT BUT EASY PEASY PUDDING

## INGREDIENTS

Serves 4
Preparation time 10 minutes
Chilling time 1 hour or more

6 tsp Fairtrade instant coffee
300ml (10fl oz) double cream
200g (7oz) packet of biscuits, such as
  Fairtrade Double Chocolate Chip

Biscuits, or plain, chocolate, or
  nutty biscuits
30g (1oz) Fairtrade chocolate, chopped,
  or a few grated Fairtrade nuts for
  decoration, if desired

## METHOD

**Dissolve** the instant coffee in 120ml (4fl oz) of hot water to make a very strong cup of coffee, and leave to cool.

**Whip** the double cream until stiff.

**Dip** two biscuits in the coffee and sandwich together with cream.

**Repeat** with the rest of the biscuits, and then form all the biscuit cream sandwiches together in a long sausage shape on a large piece of kitchen foil.

**Cover** with the leftover whipped cream.

**Roll** the sausage shape in the foil and put it in the fridge to chill for a few hours, but longer is better.

**Remove** the foil and put the biscuit sausage on a plate.

**Decorate** with chopped nuts or chocolate or both. To serve, cut the slices on the diagonal.

*Tip* For grown-ups, use sherry instead of the coffee.

**Sue Ashmore** from Hepscott, Northumberland

# ICKY STICKY TANGY PUDDING

## INGREDIENTS

Serves 6
Preparation time 15 minutes
Cooking time 50 minutes

### For the Sponge
175g (6oz) Fairtrade dried pitted organic
  dates, chopped
175ml (6fl oz) water
1 tsp bicarbonate of soda
60g (2oz) butter

2 tbsp Fairtrade Seville orange
  marmalade
150g (5½oz) Fairtrade Demerara sugar,
  or Fairtrade soft brown sugar
2 large eggs, beaten
200g (7oz) self-raising flour, sifted

### For the Sauce
100ml (3½fl oz) double cream
200g (7oz) Fairtrade Demerara sugar
125g (4½oz) butter

## METHOD

**Preheat** the oven to 150°C/300°F/Gas Mark 2. Grease and flour a 20cm (8in) round cake tin.

**Place** the dates in a pan with the water and the bicarbonate of soda and bring it to the boil for 2–3 minutes until the dates soften.

**Remove** from the heat. Add the butter and stir until it melts.

**Mix** in the marmalade, making sure it melts. Add the sugar and stir in the beaten eggs.

**Fold** the flour in carefully. The mixture should look like a thick batter.

**Pour** the mixture into the prepared cake tin and place in the oven. Check after 50 minutes to see if a skewer inserted in the middle of the cake comes out clean. If not, bake for up to another 10 minutes and test again.

**Make** the sauce by placing the cream, sugar, and butter in a saucepan. Gently heat the mixture, stirring all the time to dissolve the sugar. Bring to the boil and turn off the heat.

**Cool** the sauce slightly before serving over generous portions of the sponge.

**Judges' note** This is delicious and the peel in the orange marmalade really gives it bite. You could try adding 1 tsp of strong Fairtrade coffee to the marmalade if you like. You could also serve this with Fairtrade vanilla ice cream or double cream.

**Sally Northeast** from Southsea, Hampshire

# ROCKY ROAD BROWNIES

## INGREDIENTS

Makes 18
Preparation time 20 minutes
Cooking time 35-40 minutes

200g (7oz) unsalted butter
150g (5½oz) Fairtrade milk chocolate
500g (1lb 2oz) caster sugar

150g (5½oz) plain flour
60g (2oz) Fairtrade cocoa
5 large eggs, beaten
150g (5½oz) small marshmallows
100g (3½oz) of walnuts, optional
100g (3½oz) Fairtrade chocolate
   chips, optional

## METHOD

**Preheat** the oven to 180°C/350°F/Gas Mark 4.

**Line** a 20 x 30cm (8 x 12in) tin with baking parchment.

**Melt** the butter and chocolate together slowly in a bowl placed over a pan of barely simmering water.

**Mix** the sugar, flour, and cocoa together in a bowl.

**Stir** in the melted butter and chocolate mixture.

**Mix** in the eggs, marshmallows, and any other extras, such as the walnuts or chocolate chips.

**Turn** the brownie mixture into the tin and bake for around 35 minutes.

**Remove** from the oven, allow to cool, and cut into squares.

*Tip* For a really squidgy brownie, bake for a slightly shorter length of time.

**Miss S Dodd** from Ipswich, Suffolk

# HONEY CAKE

## INGREDIENTS

Serves 8
Preparation 20 minutes
Cooking time 40 minutes

125g (4½oz) butter or margarine
125g (4½oz) Fairtrade soft brown sugar
125g (4½oz) each Fairtrade honey and
   Fairtrade golden syrup, or 250g (9oz)
   Fairtrade honey

190g (7oz) plain flour
1 tsp bicarbonate of soda
125g (4½oz) Fairtrade dried mixed fruit
1 large egg, beaten
50g (1¾oz) walnuts, roughly chopped

## METHOD

**Preheat** the oven to 180°C/350°F/Gas Mark 4. Line a shallow 20cm (8in) tin with baking parchment or a cake liner.

**Melt** the butter, sugar, and honey (and syrup if using) together in a saucepan on a moderate heat, or in the microwave. Allow to cool slightly.

**Stir** the flour, bicarbonate of soda, and mixed fruit into the melted ingredients.

**Add** the egg and mix well.

**Sprinkle** the walnuts over the cake.

**Bake** for about 40 minutes. The cake will rise then fall – don't worry. Its consistency is more like a brownie than a sponge cake. It should be set but still springy.

**Allow** to cool in the tin.

*Tip* If you like a really strong honey taste, use just Fairtrade honey, but for a milder flavour use Fairtrade honey and Fairtrade golden syrup together. This is a lovely, moist cake and is difficult to resist.

# MORE LIKE A MOIST BROWNIE THAN A SPONGE CAKE

**Mrs Helme** from Tillington, Hereford

# LAVENDER ICE CREAM

## INGREDIENTS

Serves 4
Preparation time 15 minutes
Cooking time 7 minutes

300ml (10fl oz) whole milk
300ml (10fl oz) double cream

4 large egg yolks
110g (4oz) Fairtrade lavender sugar

## METHOD

**Put** the egg yolks in a large bowl with the sugar and whisk until fluffy, pale, and thick. Set aside.

**Gently** heat the milk in a saucepan until just below boiling. Pour the milk onto the egg mixture whisking continuously. Pour it all back into the (cleaned) saucepan and place over a gentle heat. Stir continuously with a wooden spoon until the mixture thickens and coats the back of the spoon, taking care not to let it boil, as the mixture will scramble.

**Remove** from the heat and cool completely, stirring from time to time to prevent a skin forming. In another bowl whisk the cream lightly and stir into the custard mixture. Pour into an ice-cream container and place in the freezer until half frozen.

**Remove** from the freezer, tip into a bowl, and whisk again. Return it to the container and refreeze.

*Tip* You can also make this recipe using an ice-cream maker if you have one, following the manufacturer's instructions.

**Judges' note** You can obtain organic lavender sugar from Steenbergs Organic. See page 219 for details. If you prefer not to have the flecks of whole lavender, you can strain the custard while it is hot, but you will lose some of the intensity of flavour.

**Miss L Viggers** from King's Lynn, Peterborough

# MANGO YOGHURT BRÛLÉES

## INGREDIENTS

Serves 4
Preparation time 10 minutes
Cooking time 3 minutes

500g (1 lb 2oz) tub of Greek yoghurt
2 ripe passion fruit

2 tbsp Fairtrade runny honey
1 ripe Fairtrade mango, peeled, stone
   removed, and diced
4 tbsp Fairtrade muscovado sugar

## METHOD

**Preheat** the grill to its highest setting. Mix the yoghurt with the juice and seeds of the passion fruit and the runny honey, and set aside.

**Place** the diced mango in four ovenproof ramekins.

**Top** with the yoghurt mixture.

**Sprinkle** each ramekin with one tbsp of muscovado sugar and flash under the grill until the sugar caramelizes.

**Leave** to cool before serving.

# A ZINGY NEW TWIST ON A TRADITIONAL FAVOURITE

**Mrs J Raine** from Bishop Auckland, County Durham

# FAIR FRUIT 'N' CRISP DESSERT

## INGREDIENTS

Serves 4
Preparation time 30 minutes
Cooking time 5–8 minutes

**Fruit**
2 or 3 Fairtrade eating apples
  (250g/9oz), peeled, cored, and
  chopped
8 dried Fairtrade apricots, chopped
100ml (3½fl oz) Fruit Passion orange
  juice or other Fairtrade juice

¼ tsp Fairtrade ground cinnamon, or
  Fairtrade ground ginger (optional)

**Crisp**
100g (3½oz) Fairtrade orange milk
  chocolate, chopped
2 tsp Fairtrade blossom honey
120g (4oz) Fairtrade vine fruit muesli
40g (1½oz) mixture of Fairtrade nuts,
  finely chopped

## METHOD

**Place** the fruit in a small pan along with the juice and spice if you are using it. Bring to the boil and simmer for five minutes until soft. Set aside to cool.

**Melt** the chocolate and honey for the crisp gently in a small pan on a low heat.

**Stir** in the muesli and nuts until well coated, and leave to cool.

**Divide** half the fruit between four small glasses, then top with half the crisp, and repeat.

**Chill** and serve with Ben & Jerry's Fairtrade vanilla ice cream.

**Marion Hill** from London

# BANANA BUTTERSCOTCH PUDDING

## INGREDIENTS

Serves 4-6
Preparation time 20 minutes
Cooking time 30-40 minutes

**Pudding**
125g (4½oz) plain flour
3 tsp baking powder
125g (4½oz) caster sugar
1 large egg, beaten

1 Fairtrade banana, mashed
225ml (8fl oz) milk
1 tsp Fairtrade vanilla extract
100g (3½oz) melted butter

**Topping**
115g (4oz) Fairtrade soft brown sugar
1 tbsp Fairtrade golden syrup

## METHOD

**Preheat** the oven to 180°F/350°F/Gas Mark 4. Sift the flour and baking powder in a large bowl and stir in the sugar.

**Mix** together the beaten egg, mashed banana, and milk, and add to the flour mixture. Beat until evenly mixed. Pour the mixture into a 1.5litre (2¾pint) pie dish. Place the dish on a baking tray. Now make the topping.

**Put** the brown sugar, golden syrup, and 150ml (5fl oz) boiling water in saucepan and bring to the boil.

**Drizzle** the topping over the pudding and place it in the oven.

**Cook** for 30-40 minutes.

# CRUNCHY TOPPING, SMOOTH BUTTERSCOTCH INSIDE

**Mrs Cindy Forbes** from Dundee

# WHITE CHOCOLATE CAKES

## INGREDIENTS

Makes 9 squares
Preparation time 10 minutes
Cooking time 30–35 minutes
plus cooling

### Cake
50g (1¾oz) butter, softened
50g (1¾oz) Fairtrade granulated sugar
1 tsp Fairtrade vanilla extract
2 medium eggs

100g (3½oz) self-raising flour
200g (7oz) Fairtrade white chocolate,
  finely chopped
100g (3½oz) walnuts, chopped

### Topping
200g (7oz) Fairtrade white chocolate
50g (1¾oz) walnuts for decoration,
  chopped

## METHOD

**Preheat** the oven to 160°C/325°F/Gas Mark 3. Grease a high-sided 16cm (7in) square tin with butter. Line it with a strip of greaseproof paper and set it aside.

**Cream** the butter, sugar, and vanilla in a bowl with an electric beater until smooth and creamy.

**Add** the eggs one by one, beating well after each addition.

**Fold** in the flour, then the chocolate and the walnuts.

**Spread** the mixture in the tin and bake for 30–35 minutes or until set.

**Cool** in the tin for 10 minutes before turning out.

**For** the topping, melt the white chocolate in a bowl placed over gently simmering water, then pour it over the cooled cake. Allow it to set before decorating with walnuts and cutting in to squares.

*Tip* You may find the white chocolate cakes are already sweet enough without the icing.

# DELICIOUS WITH ICING OR ABSOLUTELY PLAIN

**Monica Tai** from West Chinook Primary School Cookery Club, West Chinnock, Crewkerne

# BANANA CRUMBLE CAKE

## INGREDIENTS

Makes 12
Preparation time 20 minutes
Cooking time 25–30 minutes

Topping
55g (2oz) Fairtrade golden granulated
 sugar
30g (1oz) plain flour
½ tsp Fairtrade ground cinnamon
30g (1oz) salted butter

Cake
45g (1½oz) salted butter, softened
75g (2½oz) Fairtrade golden granulated
 sugar
1 large egg
½ tsp Fairtrade vanilla extract
75 ml (2½fl oz) semi-skimmed milk
110g (4oz) plain flour
1 tsp baking powder
3 medium (or 2 large) Fairtrade bananas,
 sliced

## METHOD

**Preheat** the oven to 190°C/ 375°F/Gas Mark 5. Lightly grease a 20cm (8in) square baking tin.

**Make** the topping first. Mix the sugar, flour, and cinnamon in a bowl, then rub in the butter, until the mixture resembles breadcrumbs.

**For** the cake, cream together the butter and sugar in another bowl.

**Mix** in the egg, vanilla, and milk.

**Sift** together the flour and baking powder. Then add the flour mixture to the wet ingredients and stir until just combined.

**Spread** the batter evenly in the prepared tin.

**Place** the banana slices evenly over the batter, then finish with the crumb topping. Bake for 25–30 minutes or until a knife placed in the centre comes out clean.

**Serve** with your favourite Fairtrade coffee – enjoy!

**Summer Hawkins** from London

# SCRUMMY CRUMBLE

## INGREDIENTS

Serves 4
Preparation time 10 minutes plus soaking
Cooking time 25 minutes

2 cooking apples, peeled, cored, and diced
250g (9oz) Fairtrade dried mixed fruit

100ml (3½fl oz) Fairtrade red wine
50g (1¾oz) Fairtrade brazil nuts, walnuts, and almonds
2 tbsp Fairtrade dark muscovado sugar
60g (2oz) digestive biscuits, crushed
1 tsp Fairtrade ground cinnamon
Double cream to serve

## METHOD

**Preheat** the oven to 180°C/350°F/Gas Mark 4. Place the apple in a small pan with 2 tbsp of water. Cover and cook for 3–5 minutes until soft, then crush with a fork. In another bowl soak the dried fruit in red wine until it is soft, and add to the apple purée. Place in a 20–25cm (8–10in) diameter ovenproof dish.

**Grind** the nuts to a coarse powder in a processor. Mix with the sugar, biscuit crumbs, and cinnamon.

**Scatter** this mixture over the fruit. Bake in the oven for about 25 minutes until the topping is golden brown.

**Serve** hot with cream and enjoy!

*Tip* For a chunkier texture, chop the nuts into coarse pieces.

# CRUNCHY, NUTTY, SWEET, AND PACKED WITH FRUIT

**Susan Roche** from Upper Sheringham, Norfolk

# RICH MOCHA CAKE

## INGREDIENTS

Serves 12
Preparation time 20 minutes
Cooking time 45 minutes

250g (9oz) Fairtrade dark chocolate,
  broken into pieces
100ml (3½fl oz) Fairtrade strong coffee
100g (3½oz) butter

6 large eggs, whites and yolks separated
75g (2½oz) Fairtrade brown sugar
40g (1½oz) plain flour
50ml (2fl oz) crème fraîche
50ml (2fl oz) Fairtrade coffee liqueur
3 tbsp Fairtrade cocoa
1 tbsp icing sugar

## METHOD

**Preheat** the oven to 150°C (300°F). Grease and base-line a 20cm (8in) spring-release cake tin.

**Melt** 150g (5½oz) of the chocolate in a bowl over a pan of simmering water, with the coffee.

**Add** the butter and mix well. Remove from the heat.

**Beat** the yolks with the sugar in another bowl until light in colour.

**Add** the melted chocolate, and then the flour.

**Beat** the egg whites until stiff, and then fold them into the chocolate mixture.

**Pour** the mixture into the prepared cake tin and place in the oven. Bake for 45 minutes.

**Meanwhile** make the icing. Melt the rest of the chocolate in a bowl over a pan of simmering water. Remove it from the heat, then stir in the crème fraîche and coffee liqueur.

**Leave** the icing to cool, stirring it from time to time.

**Take** the cake out of the tin when it has finished baking and has cooled slightly, then pour the coffee-chocolate icing all over it.

**Chill** for 10 minutes, then sprinkle with cocoa powder and icing sugar.

**Stephanie Charbine** from Sunninghill, Berkshire

# CHOCOLATE APPLE CAKE

## INGREDIENTS

Makes 16 squares
Preparation time 40 minutes
Cooking time 35 minutes

120ml (4fl oz) vegetable oil
225g (8oz) Fairtrade granulated sugar
1 large egg
175g (6oz) plain flour

40g (1½ oz) Fairtrade cocoa
1½ tsp Fairtrade ground cinnamon
1 tsp bicarbonate of soda
225g (8oz) apple purée

**Easy Chocolate Icing (optional)**
75g (3oz) Fairtrade plain chocolate
25g (1oz) unsalted butter, softened

## METHOD

**Preheat** oven to 180°C/350°F/Gas Mark 4. Grease and flour a 20 or 23cm (8 or 9in) square baking tin and set it aside.

**Beat** the oil, sugar, and egg in a large bowl until pale in colour and fluffy and set it aside.

**Sift** the flour with the cocoa powder, cinnamon, and bicarbonate of soda in another bowl.

**Stir** alternate spoonfuls of the flour mixture and the apple purée into the egg mixture.

**Pour** the mixture into the prepared tin and place in the oven.

**Bake** for 35 minutes if you are using the 20cm (8in) tin and 25 minutes if you are using the 23cm (9in) tin, or until a fine skewer inserted into the cake comes out clean.

**Turn** onto a wire rack and leave to cool.

**Melt** the chocolate for the icing in a bowl set above hot water in a saucepan over a low heat. Remove it from the heat and stir in the butter.

**Cool** for about 2 minutes or until thick enough to spread over the top of the cake.

**Refrigerate** for about 1 hour or until set. This cake can be kept, covered, for three days in the refrigerator, but should be served at room temperature.

*Tip* If you cannot find apple purée, you can make your own using three medium-sized Bramley apples.

**Helen Cox** from Liverpool

# MANGO AND PINEAPPLE PAVLOVA

## INGREDIENTS

Serves 6
Preparation time 20 minutes
Cooking time 60 minutes

3 large egg whites
175g (6oz) Fairtrade white sugar
1 tsp Fairtrade instant coffee granules

250g (9oz) fromage frais
1 Fairtrade mango, peeled, stone removed, and diced
1 small Fairtrade pineapple, peeled, cored, and cut in to chunks
2 passion fruit, pulp and seeds

## METHOD

**Preheat** the oven to 120°C/250°F/Gas Mark ½.

**Whisk** the egg whites in a large, clean, grease-free bowl until they are stiff.

**Fold** in 1 tbsp of the sugar and then gradually whisk in the remainder, 1 tbsp at a time, whisking well after each addition until the mixture is stiff and glossy. The meringue must be glossy and form peaks.

**Sieve** over the coffee and whisk it in.

**Spread** the meringue mixture over a large sheet of baking paper to form a 20cm (8in) round. Make a slight hollow in the centre of the meringue. Place it in the oven and cook for 1 hour until the meringue is crisp.

**Remove** from the oven and allow it to cool for about 10 minutes. Peel off the paper, which should come off easily. If not, pop the meringue back into the oven to dry out further. Leave to cool.

**Just** before serving, fill the hollow in the top with fromage frais.

**Arrange** the mango and pineapple on top, then drizzle the passion fruit pulp and seeds over the fruit. Eat immediately!

**Gill Heels** from Barrow-in-Furness, Cumbria

# CHOCOLATE MOUSSE

## INGREDIENTS

Serves 4
Preparation time 20 minutes
Chilling time 1 hour

50g (1¾oz) caster sugar
3 large egg yolks

100g (3½oz) Fairtrade dark chocolate,
 roughly chopped
50g (1¾oz) Fairtrade milk chocolate,
 roughly chopped
150ml (5oz) double cream

## METHOD

**Whisk** the sugar and egg yolks for about 5 minutes in a bowl over simmering water until they are thick and creamy, and set aside.

**Melt** the chocolate in another bowl over a small pan of barely simmering water. Once it has melted let it cool slightly before folding it into the egg yolks and sugar. Set aside.

**Whip** the cream in another bowl until it forms soft peaks. Then add a spoonful to the chocolate and beat in to loosen the mixture.

**Fold** the rest into the chocolate and pour it into 4 glasses for serving. Chill for an hour or until you are ready to serve it.

*Tip* You could serve this with some extra grated dark chocolate on the top and a dollop of crème fraîche or whipped cream.

# A DARK, DIVINE, SIMPLY SINFUL PLEASURE

**Craig Wilson** from Ellon, Aberdeenshire

# DRIZZLED BANANA SUNSHINE SURPRISE

## INGREDIENTS

Makes 18-24 pieces
Preparation time 5 minutes
Cooking time 20-25 minutes plus
cooling

175g (6oz) butter or margarine, softened
175g (6oz) caster sugar, plus 1 tbsp
1 tsp Fairtrade vanilla extract

175g (6oz) self-raising flour
200g (7oz) porridge oats,
25g (1oz) Fairtrade raisins
2 Fairtrade ripe bananas, peeled and
diced
175g (6oz) Fairtrade milk or dark
chocolate, chopped

## METHOD

**Preheat** oven to 200°C/400°F/Gas Mark 6. Grease a 20 x 30cm (8 x 12in) baking tin with butter and line with a strip of greaseproof paper.

**Cream** the butter, 175g (6oz) of the sugar and the vanilla extract in a bowl with an electric beater until smooth and creamy.

**Cut** or rub in the flour and oats gently, without over-handling the mixture, to make it crumbly.

**Press** the mixture into the prepared tin. Set the raisins into the top of the mixture, so as not to burn, then top with the sliced banana.

**Sprinkle** with the remaining sugar. Place in the oven and bake for 20-25 minutes until golden brown.

**Remove** from the oven and allow to cool completely in the tin. Meanwhile, carefully melt the chocolate in a bowl placed over a pan of gently simmering water.

**Drizzle** the melted chocolate over the cooled biscuit. Once it has set cut it into 18-24 pieces.

*Tip* This recipe is especially delicious with a glass of cold milk. These keep well in an airtight container.

**Megan Palfreyman** from Sunninghill, Berkshire

# FAIRTRADE TIFFIN

## INGREDIENTS

Serves 16
Preparation time 10 minutes
Cooking time 10 minutes plus cooling
and setting

100g (3½oz) butter, diced
100g (3½oz) Fairtrade muscovado sugar
100g (3½oz) Fairtrade wild blossom
  honey
50g (1¾oz) Fairtrade cocoa powder

50g (1¾oz) Fairtrade sultanas
50g (1¾oz) Fairtrade raisins
50g (1¾oz) Fairtrade brazil nuts,
  chopped
50g (1¾oz) walnuts, chopped
300g (10oz) Fairtrade vine fruit muesli
200g (7oz) Fairtrade dark chocolate,
  chopped

## METHOD

**Grease** a 20cm (8in) square tin with butter and line with a strip of greaseproof paper. Set aside.

**Place** the butter, sugar, honey, and cocoa in a pan and melt gently over a low heat, stirring.

**Bring** to the boil, and stir in the fruit and nuts. Cook for 5 minutes, stirring.

**Place** the muesli in a large bowl and pour the fruit mixture into the centre.

**Mix** well and spread into the prepared tin. Allow to cool.

**Melt** the chocolate meanwhile in a bowl set over a saucepan of gently simmering water.

**Pour** the chocolate over the tiffin and smooth it over. Allow it to set before cutting into squares or slices.

**Margaret Weeks** from Gloucester

# CHOCOLATE CHERRY BITES

## INGREDIENTS

Makes 18
Preparation time 15 minutes
Cooking time 35 minutes

vegetable oil, for brushing
175g (6oz) Fairtrade milk or plain
  chocolate, chopped

50g (1¾oz) unsalted butter, diced
100g (3½oz) caster sugar
1 medium egg, beaten
100g (3½oz) desiccated coconut
50g (1¾oz) natural glacé cherries
50g (1¾oz) Fairtrade sultanas

## METHOD

**Preheat** the oven to 160°C/325°F/Gas Mark 3. Line a 16 x 25cm (6 x 10in) deep baking tin with kitchen foil and then brush it with oil.

**Melt** the chocolate in a bowl set over a saucepan of gently simmering water.

**Pour** into the prepared tin and spread evenly over the base. Set aside or chill for 5 minutes.

**Cream** the butter and sugar in a large bowl with an electric beater until smooth and creamy.

**Add** the egg and mix well. Then stir in all the remaining ingredients.

**Pour** the mixture into the tin and spread over the chocolate. Place in the oven and bake for 35-40 minutes until golden and firm to the touch.

**Allow** to cool before turning out, peeling off the foil, and cutting into squares.

# TART YET SWEET CHERRIES BAKED IN CHOCOLATE

**Mrs H Julian-Jones** from Wokingham

# KNICKERBOCKER GLORY

## INGREDIENTS

Serves 4–6 depending on size of
serving glasses
Preparation time 20 minutes

1 small Fairtrade mango, peeled, stone
  removed, and chopped
225g (8oz) raspberries
3 tbsp icing sugar, sifted

4 kiwi fruit, peeled and chopped
400g (14oz) fromage frais
Grated rind of 1 Fairtrade lemon
1 tbsp Fairtrade clear honey
2 medium-sized Fairtrade bananas
4 scoops Fairtrade vanilla ice cream
Sweet finger biscuits or wafers to serve

## METHOD

**Place** mango in a blender. Blend until smooth, remove, and set aside. Rinse the blender.

**Fold** the icing sugar into the raspberries in a bowl, then place in the blender and blend to a purée.
Remove and set aside. Rinse out the blender. Place the kiwi fruit into the blender and blend until smooth.
Set aside.

**Mix** together the fromage frais, lemon rind, and honey in another bowl.

**Layer** the fromage frais mixture in four tall glasses, alternating with the fruit purées.

**Peel** and slice the bananas and arrange over the fruit purées. Top with a scoop of ice cream.

**Serve** with sweet finger biscuits or wafers.

**Mrs A J Costello** from Gateshead, Tyne and Wear

# POFESEN

## INGREDIENTS

Serves 6
Preparation time 25 minutes plus resting time
Cooking time 10 minutes

**Pancake batter**
110g (4oz) plain flour
A pinch of salt
1 tsp fast-action yeast
2 large eggs
200ml (7fl oz) milk, mixed with 90ml (3fl oz) water

**Jam sandwiches**
2 tsp Fairtrade vanilla extract
1 tsp Fairtrade ground cinnamon
1 tsp Fairtrade rum
200g (7oz) plum jam
12 slices thinly sliced white bread, crusts cut off
575ml (1 pint) Fairtrade white wine
1 tbsp Fairtrade white sugar
2 tbsp vegetable oil, for frying
Icing sugar, for dusting

## METHOD

**Make** the pancake batter. Sift the flour with the salt into a large bowl. Stir in the yeast. Make a well in the centre and break in the eggs. Gradually add the milk, whisking the flour in until the batter is smooth. Leave in a warm place for 30 minutes.

**Stir** 1 tsp of the vanilla extract, all the cinnamon, and the rum into the plum jam.

**Make** six jam sandwiches with the bread and the spiced jam.

**Cut** the sandwiches in half diagonally and set them aside.

**Pour** the white wine into a shallow bowl or basin. Add the remaining tsp of vanilla extract and the tbsp of sugar and stir until the sugar has dissolved. Set it aside.

**Heat** the oil in a large frying pan. Dip each jam sandwich triangle into the white wine mixture and then coat in the pancake mixture.

**Fry** them in batches over a medium to high heat 1–2 minutes on each side until puffed up and golden brown. Lift them out and put them on a tray lined with kitchen paper to drain for a minute or so.

**Sprinkle** with the icing sugar just before serving.

*Tip* Pofesen can be eaten warm or cold. This is an old family recipe and my grandmother and my mother always made it at Easter.

**Mrs Elizabeth Tompkinson** from Leigh-on-Sea, Essex

# BITTER CHOCOLATE, APRICOT, AND ALMOND TART

## INGREDIENTS

Serves 6-8
Preparation time 20 minutes
Cooking time 1 hour, plus
18 minutes baking blind

170g (6oz) butter
115g (4oz) plain flour

400g (14oz) tin apricot halves, drained
100g (3½oz) Fairtrade dark chocolate,
  broken into chunks
110g (4oz) caster sugar
2 large eggs
75g (2½oz) ground almonds, mixed with
75g (2½oz) Madeira cake crumbs

## METHOD

**Make** the pastry by rubbing 55g (2oz) of the butter into the flour. Add enough iced water to make a dough. Knead briefly to smooth out, then roll into a ball, wrap in cling film, and rest in the fridge for 30 minutes.

**Preheat** the oven to 180°C/350°F/Gas Mark 4. Grease a 23cm (9in) tart tin. Roll out the pastry, line the dish with it, and chill again for 30 minutes. Prick the base all over with a fork, line with baking parchment, weigh down with baking beans and bake for 12 minutes. Remove the beans and paper, then return to the oven for a further 5-7 minutes to dry out.

**Put** the well drained apricots cut-side down in the pastry case and scatter over the chocolate chunks.

**Cream** the remaining butter with the sugar in a large bowl using an electric whisk until light and fluffy. Slowly beat in the eggs one at a time taking care not to curdle the mixture.

**Fold** in the almond and crumb mixture and spoon it over the chocolate and apricots. Smooth down lightly. Bake for 40 minutes or until the tart is firm and golden. Allow to cool slightly before serving warm.

# DELECTABLE WITH CREAM OR VANILLA ICE CREAM

**Marie-Claude Whitaker** from Groombridge, Kent

# STRAWBERRY MERINGUE STACK

## INGREDIENTS

Serves 4
Preparation time 25 minutes
Cooking time 2 hours plus overnight

2 large egg whites
115g (4oz) caster sugar
1 tsp Fairtrade cocoa

25g (1oz) Fairtrade dark chocolate
300g (10oz) Greek yoghurt, drained of
    liquid, or softly whipped double cream
300g (10oz) strawberries, washed,
    hulled, and halved

## METHOD

**Make** the meringues in advance the night before. Preheat the oven to 140°C/275°F/Gas Mark 1.

**Line** an oven tray with baking parchment and mark out two rectangles approx 10 x 20cm (4 x 8in).

**Whisk** the egg whites into a clean, grease-free bowl until stiff. Add the sugar a tablespoon at a time, whisking well after each addition to make a thick, glossy meringue.

**Sift** over the cocoa and carefully fold in using a metal spoon.

**Spoon** the meringue into a piping bag and pipe 2 rectangles onto the baking parchment using a zigzag motion. Or you can simply spread the meringue with a spoon onto the paper.

**Bake** for 2 hours, then switch off the oven and leave the meringues inside overnight.

**Melt** the chocolate in a small bowl over a pan of gently simmering water. Using a teaspoon, drizzle the melted chocolate over one of the meringue rectangles. Leave to harden.

**Place** the undecorated meringue on a presentation plate, spread over the yoghurt or softly whipped cream, top with the strawberries and then the chocolate-drizzled meringue.

# IMPRESSIVE, YET SIMPLICITY ITSELF TO PREPARE

**Miss K M Manouch** from Chichester

# GLUTEN-FREE CHOCOLATE CAKE

## INGREDIENTS

Serves 12
Preparation time 20 minutes
Cooking time 40-50 minutes

### Cake mixture
125g (4½oz) butter
50g (1¾oz) Fairtrade granulated sugar
125g (4½oz) Fairtrade dark chocolate

300g (10oz) ground almonds
2 large eggs, separated

### Topping
200g (7oz) Fairtrade chocolate
100g (3½oz) butter
100g (3½oz) Fairtrade strawberry jam, or
   Fairtrade marmalade

## METHOD

**Preheat** the oven to 180°C/350°F/Gas Mark 4. Grease a loose-bottomed 20cm (8in) round spring-release cake tin and set aside.

**Cream** the butter with sugar together in a large bowl until light and fluffy.

**Melt** the plain chocolate in a bowl placed over a saucepan of simmering water.

**Stir** the ground almonds, egg yolk, and melted chocolate into the sugar and butter mixture.

**Whisk** the egg whites until they are stiff. Fold a little egg white into the cake mixture to loosen it and then gently fold in the rest.

**Spoon** the batter into the prepared tin and bake for approximately 40-50 minutes or until a skewer plunged into the middle of the cake comes out clean.

**Remove** the cake from the oven and allow it to cool. Meanwhile make the topping by melting the 200g (7oz) chocolate with the 100g (3½oz) butter. Allow it to cool to a coating consistency.

**Spread** the jam over the top and sides of the cake when the cake and the topping are both cool enough to use. Then spread the top and sides of the cake with the chocolate topping.

**Place** in the fridge to set.

*Tip* If you prefer, you could used sieved apricot jam instead of the strawberry jam. You could serve this cake with fresh raspberries or chocolate-dipped strawberries.

**Ursula Dove** from Bobbersmill, Nottingham

# TRIPLE CHOCOLATE CRUNCH BARS

## INGREDIENTS

Serves 8
Preparation time 5 minutes
Baking 20-25 minutes plus cooling
250g (9oz) butter, softened
200g (7oz) caster sugar
3 medium eggs, beaten
200g (7oz) self-raising flour

50g (1¾oz) Fairtrade cocoa powder
50g (1¾oz) Fairtrade dark chocolate, chopped
50g (1¾oz) Fairtrade milk chocolate, chopped
50g (1¾oz) Fairtrade white chocolate, chopped

## METHOD

**Preheat** the oven to 200°C/400°F/Gas Mark 6. Grease the baking tin with butter and line with a strip of greaseproof paper.

**Cream** the butter and sugar in a bowl using an electric beater until smooth and creamy.

**Add** the beaten eggs, a little at a time, beating continuously.

**Fold** in the flour, cocoa powder, and all the chocolate, and spread into the prepared tin.

**Bake** for 20-25 minutes until the sides have set and the centre is still a little sticky. Remove, cover with foil, and allow to cool before cutting into squares.

**Cut** into eight generous slices and enjoy!

*Tip* If you prefer milk or dark chocolate you could just use 150g (5oz) of your favourite Fairtrade brand. Or, if you have bought 150g (5oz) bars of each, you can melt the remainder and serve it on top of the bars. To serve, you can also dust the bars with a sprinkling of Fairtrade cocoa.

**Mrs F Murphy** Tuxford, Newark

# COFFEETIME MUFFINS

## INGREDIENTS

Makes 12 muffins
Preparation time 20 minutes
Cooking time 25 minutes

150g (5½oz) sultanas
4 tbsp Fairtrade coffee liqueur or Kahlúa
400g (14oz) self-raising flour
1 tsp bicarbonate of soda

75g (2½oz) walnuts
6 tbsp Fairtrade instant coffee
175g (6oz) Fairtrade Demerara sugar
2 large eggs, slightly beaten
100g (3½oz) butter, melted and left to
  cool slightly
500g (1lb 2oz) tub Greek yoghurt
1 ripe Fairtrade banana, mashed

## METHOD

**Soak** the sultanas in the coffee liqueur. Preheat the oven to 200°C/400°F/Gas Mark 6. Line a 12-hole muffin tin with paper baking cases.

**Sift** together the flour and bicarbonate of soda. Mix in the walnuts, coffee, and sugar.

**Whisk** the beaten eggs with the cooled butter, yoghurt, and banana in another bowl. Stir this quickly into the flour mixture but don't overbeat – small lumps of flour are fine.

**Tip** in the soaked sultanas and give the mixture a few more stirs to finish mixing.

**Spoon** the mixture into the paper cases. The muffin cups will be very full.

**Place** in the oven and bake for 25 minutes until risen and golden.

*Tip* Enjoy with a cup of your favourite Fairtrade coffee.

# TAKE THE TIME TO RELAX AND ENJOY A MUFFIN

**Yvonne Allison** from Meanwood, Leeds

# WHITE CHOCOLATE CHEESECAKE

## INGREDIENTS

Serves 6
Preparation time 25 minutes
Cooking time 50 minutes, plus
chilling overnight

150g (5½oz) digestive biscuits
50g (1¾oz) butter
200g (7oz) Fairtrade white chocolate

500g (1lb 2oz) ricotta cheese
2 large eggs
100g (3½oz) Fairtrade dark chocolate,
  melted
4 tbsp double cream
fresh raspberries, to serve

## METHOD

**Preheat** the oven to 160°C/325°F/Gas Mark 3. Base-line a 20cm (8in) springform cake tin with baking parchment and grease the sides. Place the biscuits in a sturdy plastic bag and bash with a rolling pin to crumble them.

**Melt** the butter in a small saucepan and stir in the biscuit crumbs. Press evenly and firmly into the cake tin, smoothing over with the back of a wooden spoon. Chill in the fridge.

**Melt** the white chocolate in a bowl set over a pan of barely simmering water, stirring occasionally.

**Beat** the ricotta and eggs in another bowl until smooth, then mix in the melted white chocolate. Spoon the mixture onto the biscuit base. Put the baking tin on a baking sheet. Bake for 45 minutes until set. Remove from the oven and leave to cool.

**When** the cheesecake has cooled melt the dark chocolate as above and stir in the cream. Spread evenly over the cheesecake. Chill, preferably overnight.

**Remove** the outside ring to serve, and lift the base onto a serving plate. Serve with fresh raspberries.

**Mrs Debra Williams** from Cardiff

# PANACOTTA WITH PORT SAUCE

## INGREDIENTS

Serves 4–6
Preparation time 7 minutes
plus setting time
Cooking time 10 minutes

3½ gelatine leaves
600ml (1 pint) double cream

1 Fairtrade vanilla pod, split
50g (1¾oz) caster sugar

Port Sauce
100ml (3½fl oz) port
50g (1¾oz) Fairtrade granulated sugar
1 Fairtrade cinnamon stick, broken in half

## METHOD

**Soak** the gelatine leaves in cold water in a roasting tin for 5–10 minutes.

**Gently** heat the cream in a saucepan with the vanilla pod to just below boiling point. Add the sugar and stir until completely dissolved and take off the heat.

**One** by one drain the gelatine sheets and squeeze out any excess water with your hands. Stir into the hot cream.

**Divide** the mixture between 4–6 ramekin dishes or metal dariole moulds. Leave to cool, cover with cling film, and chill in the fridge overnight or until set.

**Place** all the port sauce ingredients into a small saucepan over a low heat. Heat gently until the sugar has dissolved. Raise the heat and boil for about 5 minutes until syrupy. Allow to cool. Remove the cinnamon stick before serving.

**Briefly** dip each dish into a bowl of hot water before serving to loosen the edges and turn out onto a plate. Serve with a little port sauce.

# A CLASSIC SUMMER PUDDING THAT CAN BE MADE AHEAD

**Mrs V Leek** from Birmingham

# FAIR CHOCOLATE FUDGE CAKE

## INGREDIENTS

Serves 6
Preparation time 30 minutes
Cooking time 45 minutes

50g (1¾oz) Fairtrade cocoa
150g (5½oz) butter, softened
150g (5½oz) caster sugar
150g (5½oz) self-raising flour
2 tsp baking powder

4 large eggs, beaten

For the icing
50g (1¾oz) Fairtrade dark chocolate,
  broken into small pieces
25g (1oz) butter
2 tbsp milk
225g (8oz) icing sugar, sifted

## METHOD

**Preheat** the oven to 170°C/325°F/Gas Mark 3. Grease and line a 20cm (8in) round cake tin with baking parchment.

**Blend** the cocoa with 6 tbsp boiling water in a large bowl to make a smooth paste. Beat in the butter, sugar, sieved flour and baking powder, and the eggs. Mix until combined with an electric hand mixer.

**Spoon** into the prepared tin and level the top. Bake for 40–45 minutes until a skewer inserted in the middle of the cake comes out clean. Leave the cake in the tin to cool for 15 minutes, then unmould and finish cooling on a cake rack.

**Meanwhile** place the chocolate, butter, and milk in a bowl over a pan of barely simmering water to melt. Stir to combine and remove from the heat. Sift over the icing sugar and beat well to mix. Add a drop or two of milk if the icing is too thick.

**Spread** the icing over the top and sides of the cake in rough swirls.

*Tip* You could decorate the cake with grated Fairtrade plain chocolate or a dusting of Fairtrade cocoa. Enjoy a slice with a cup of Fairtrade tea.

**Mrs H Hardman** from Goosnargh, Preston

# INDIAN BASMATI RICE PUDDING

## INGREDIENTS

Serves 4
Preparation time 5 minutes
Cooking time approximately
15 minutes

85g (3 oz) caster sugar

570ml (1 scant pint) milk
1 Fairtrade vanilla pod, slit open
200g (7oz) Fairtrade basmati rice
110ml (4fl oz) double cream
4 tbsp Fairtrade soft brown sugar

## METHOD

**Preheat** the grill. Place the caster sugar, milk, and vanilla pod into a pan and bring to the boil.

**Add** the rice, reduce the heat, and simmer gently for 8–10 minutes.

**Add** the cream and simmer for a further 4–5 minutes until the rice is tender. Remove the vanilla pod.

**Divide** the rice pudding between 4 heat-proof serving bowls, and sprinkle over the brown sugar.

**Slide** the bowls under the hot grill, and leave until the sugar is bubbling and caramelized. Alternatively, if you have one, you could use a kitchen blowtorch to glaze the rice pudding.

**Serve** immediately.

# PINEAPPLE UPSIDE-DOWN CAKE

## INGREDIENTS

Serves 6
Preparation time 30 minutes
Cooking time 45–50 minutes

175g (6oz) Fairtrade granulated sugar
4 Fairtrade dates, chopped
4 Fairtrade dried apricots, chopped
I small ripe Fairtrade pineapple, peeled,
   cored, and cut in 5 slices
50g (1¾oz) butter

Cake mixture
110g (4oz) butter, softened
I medium Fairtrade orange, zest and juice
110g (4oz) caster sugar
2 large eggs
140g (5oz) self-raising flour

## METHOD

**Preheat** the oven to 350°C/180°F/Gas Mark 4. Grease the sides of a 20cm (8in) deep-sided cake tin. (Do not use the loose-bottomed kind.)

**Heat** half the sugar gently in 280ml (10oz) water in a large, wide, heavy-bottomed saucepan and stir to dissolve. Add the dates, apricots, and pineapple. Poach slowly until soft. Turn them over occasionally to poach all the way through, but don't allow the syrup to boil.

**Remove** the pineapple and leave to drain on a cake rack with some kitchen paper underneath to catch the drips. Drain the apricots and dates and reserve any poaching liquid (see Judges' Note).

**Add** the remaining sugar and butter to the pan and melt it gently.

**Spoon** this mixture into cake tin and arrange the pineapple rings in it, squashing them up if necessary. Fill in any holes with the dates and apricots.

**To** make the cake, beat the butter with the orange zest, sugar, eggs, and flour. Gradually stir in enough orange juice to give a dropping consistency. Spoon on top of the pineapple, smooth down, then bake for 45–50 minutes until just firm.

**Turn** the cake upside down immediately onto a serving plate when it is cooked, waiting a few minutes before removing the tin.

**Judges' note** You can use any leftover poaching liquid to serve with the cake, which would also taste fabulous served warm with Fairtrade vanilla ice cream or Greek yoghurt.

**Judy Griffiths** from Dewsbury, Yorkshire

# SUNSHINE RICE PUDDING

## INGREDIENTS

Serves 4-6
Preparation time 7 minutes
Cooking time 2 hours 5 minutes

100g (3½oz) pudding rice
45g (1½oz) Fairtrade granulated sugar
1 Fairtrade orange, zest and juice
¼ Fairtrade vanilla pod, split

Pinch of salt
900ml (1½ pints) milk
100ml (3½ fl oz) double cream
1 ripe Fairtrade mango, peeled, seed
   removed, and cubed
1-2 tbsp Fairtrade honey

## METHOD

**Preheat** the oven to 170°C/340°F/Gas Mark 3½.

**Place** the rice, sugar, orange zest, vanilla pod, pinch of salt, milk, and cream in a buttered ovenproof casserole dish. Stir, cover, and bake slowly in the oven for approximately 2 hours, stirring from time to time until the rice is tender.

**Place** the orange juice and the honey in a small pan and boil until syrupy. Cool, then mix with the mango. Chill until ready to serve.

**Take** the pudding from the oven, remove the vanilla pod, and spoon into individual dishes. Cover with cling film to stop another skin forming, cool, and place in the fridge.

**Serve** the chilled rice pudding with a spoonful of the mango and syrup.

# COMFORTING RICE PUDDING WITH A TROPICAL TASTE

**Mrs V McNiven** from Ely

# TROPICAL SPICED PINEAPPLE

## INGREDIENTS

Serves 4
Preparation time 20 minutes
Cooking time 15 minutes

8 tbsp fresh pineapple juice
1 ripe Fairtrade pineapple, peeled and
   cored, sliced into 8 slices

5 tbsp Fairtrade Demerara sugar
150ml (5fl oz) gin
3 Fairtrade cardamom pods, bruised
5 juniper berries
1 Fairtrade cinnamon stick, broken into
   3 pieces

## METHOD

**Preheat** a frying pan large enough to hold the pineapple in one layer over a medium heat.

**Add** 3 tbsp pineapple juice to the pan with the pineapple rings. Sprinkle over the sugar and cook, turning frequently, until the sugar has started to caramelize around the edges.

**Pour** in the gin and bring to the boil for a minute. Add the remaining ingredients and bring back to the boil. Turn down the heat and simmer for 5 minutes.

This is divine on its own, but served with ice cream it's heavenly!

# POACHED PINEAPPLE IS A HABIT-FORMING TREAT

**Mrs Sandra Todd** from Moreton, Wirral

# BANANA RHUMBA

## INGREDIENTS

Serves 6
Preparation time 10 minutes
Cooking time 5 minutes

6 Fairtrade bananas cut in half
  lengthways
Half a Fairtrade lemon, zest and juice
2 tbsp Fairtrade Tropical Forest honey

1–2 tbsp Fairtrade white rum (or more,
  to taste)
10g (⅓oz) caster sugar
300ml (10fl oz) double cream
3 Fairtrade stem ginger cookies,
  crumbled
Fairtrade ground cinnamon, to dust

## METHOD

**Preheat** the oven to 180°C/350°F/Gas Mark 4.

**Place** the bananas on a non-stick baking tray, drizzle with lemon juice and honey, and bake for 5 minutes until warmed.

**Stir** the rum and the sugar together.

**Pour** into a large bowl with the cream and whisk with an electric beater to soft peaks.

**Place** two pieces of banana in each bowl, top with dollops of cream and crumbled cookies. Sprinkle with a pinch of cinnamon and serve immediately.

**Paul Forsyth** from St Helen's, Merseyside

# HOT DARK CHOCOLATE FONDANT

## INGREDIENTS

Serves 4
Preparation time 5 minutes
Cooking time 12 minutes

125g (4½oz) butter, diced plus extra for greasing

150g (5½oz) caster sugar, plus extra for coating the ramekins

125g (4½oz) Fairtrade dark chocolate, chopped

3 large eggs

35g (1¼oz) plain flour

## METHOD

**Preheat** the oven to 200°C/400°F/Gas Mark 6.

**Lightly** butter four 100ml (3½fl oz) ramekins or other ovenproof dishes to a maximum size of 150ml (5fl oz) each, and coat the insides of each with 1 tsp caster sugar.

**Place** the butter and chocolate in a bowl and set it over a pan of barely simmering water. Melt gently and set aside.

**Beat** the remaining caster sugar and eggs together, then mix in the flour.

**Fold** the chocolate into the egg mixture and pour into the ramekins.

**Bake** in the oven for 10–12 minutes until risen. Serve immediately.

**Judges' note** Wow! This is the chocolate-lover's dream pudding. We love it with a slick of double or whipped cream, for maximum indulgence.

# DARK CHOCOLATE HEAVEN IN A RAMEKIN

**Craig Wilson** from Ellon, Aberdeenshire

# QUICK & DELICIOUS RUM BANANAS

## INGREDIENTS

Serves 4
Preparation time 5 minutes
Cooking time 8 minutes

3 tbsp Fairtrade white rum
1 tbsp Fairtrade Demerara sugar
6 tbsp Fairtrade orange juice

1 small knob fresh ginger, peeled and
  grated
4 Fairtrade bananas, thinly sliced

Fairtrade vanilla ice cream
50g (1¾oz) Fairtrade dark chocolate,
  grated

## METHOD

**Stir** the rum, sugar, orange juice, and ginger together in a small saucepan over a medium heat until the sugar has dissolved. Boil for around 5 minutes until syrupy. Take off the the heat and allow to cool.

**Arrange** the banana slices in individual serving dishes.

**Spoon** the rum syrup over the bananas and leave for 5 minutes before serving with scoops of vanilla ice cream and the grated chocolate.

*Tip* You might like to serve this with Ben & Jerry's Fairtrade vanilla ice cream for an additional Fairtrade ingredient.

# UTTERLY YUMMY, AND MADE WITH FAIRTRADE FRUIT

**Mrs N Lowe** from Chingford, Essex

# FAIR AND PASSIONATE PINEAPPLE DESSERT WITH GROWN-UP CHOCOLATE BUTTONS

## INGREDIENTS

Serves 4
Preparation time 15 minutes
Cooking time 10 minutes

100g (3½oz) Green and Black's Maya Gold chocolate, or Fairtrade plain chocolate, broken into squares
1 tbsp shelled pistachio nuts, halved

1 tbsp Fairtrade sultanas
2 passion fruit
Juice of 1 large Fairtrade orange
1 medium-sized ripe Fairtrade pineapple, peeled and sliced into 8 slices
4 tsp Fairtrade Demerara sugar

## METHOD

Line one baking tray with baking parchment and another with foil.

Place the chocolate in a bowl set over a pan of gently simmering water. When it has melted drop teaspoons of the chocolate onto the tray lined with baking parchment. Sprinkle with the nuts and sultanas, and leave in a cool place to set.

Place the seeds and pulp of 1½ of the passion fruit with the orange juice in a blender and whizz it briefly. Sieve the mixture and stir in the remaining pulp from the leftover half passion fruit.

Preheat the grill to its highest setting. Arrange the pineapple on the foil-lined baking tray, dredge with the sugar, and immediately place under the grill until the sugar melts and caramelizes, about 4 minutes.

Serve immediately with a little of the passion fruit sauce poured round and some chocolate buttons.

*Tip* You could serve this with Ben & Jerry's Fairtrade vanilla ice cream and a sprig of mint as a garnish.

**Ann Jennings** from Stourbridge, West Midlands

# FAIRTRADE INGREDIENTS

The following Fairtrade products are available in the UK. Look out for the FAIRTRADE Mark when you are shopping for these ingredients and products. The list is constantly growing so for further details of where they are available, and the latest information, please visit www.fairtrade.org.uk

## ALE
Honey ale

## BISCUITS
All Butter Choc Chip Shortbread
All Butter Shortbread
Brazil Nut Cookies
Campaign Cookies
Caramelised Biscuit
Cherry Biscuit
Chocolate Chip Biscuit
Chocolate-Enrobed Vanilla
    Shortbread
Chocolate Chip Shortbread
Chocolate Chip Shortbread Bar
Chocolate Chip Shortbread Mini
    Bites
Chocolate Chunk Cookies
Chocolate Chunk Shortbread
Chocolate Coated Shortbread
Chocolate Coated Wafer Biscuit
    Bar
Double Chocolate Chip Cookies
Fortune Cookies

Mini Bite Chocolate Chip
    Cookies
Nutshell Biscuits
Organic Brandy Butter
    Shortbread
Organic Fireside Cookies
Organic Hazelnut Orange
    Cookies
Organic Lemon Zest Cookies
Stem Ginger Cookies
Wessex Shortbread
Vanilla Shortbread

## CHOCOLATE
Almond White Chocolate Bar
Caramel Filled Milk Chocolate
    Bar
Crispy Milk Chocolate Bar
Dark and Orange Chocolate
Dark Chocolate Bar
Fruit and Nut Dark Chocolate
Fruit and Nut Milk Chocolate
Honey Milk Chocolate Bar
Maya Gold Organic Dark

Chocolate Bar
Milk-Almonds Chocolate
Milk Chocolate Bar
Milk Chocolate Coffee Bar
Milk Chocolate Hazelnut Bar
Milk Chocolate Orange
Milk Chocolate with Broken
    Hazelnuts
Mint Dark Chocolate Bar
Organic Fairtrade Dark
    Chocolate with Chilli
Organic Milk Chocolate with
    Rose
Organic Praline Chocolate Bar
Premium Swiss Dark Chocolate
    with Mint Crisps
Rich Chocolate and Crispy Rice
    Bar
Swiss Chocolate Couverture Bar
White Chocolate Bar

## CHUTNEYS AND SAUCES
Bramley Apple Sauce with
    Kentish Cider

Cranberry Sauce with Port
Mango Chutney
Rich Chocolate Truffle Sauce
Cocoa

## COFFEE

American-style coffee
Arabica Continental Roast
Arabica Espresso Roast
Arabica full medium roast
Blend medium roast coffee
Blend mild roast coffee
Cappuccino
Coffee Granules
Coffee Mocca
Coffee Mountain
Decaffeinated Coffee
Decaffeinated instant freeze-dried Coffee
Decaffeinated Organic Roast Coffee
Espresso Blend
Espresso Coffee beans
Espresso organic roast coffee
Filter pouch coffee
Freeze-dried Arabica Coffee
Freeze-dried Coffee
Freeze-dried Instant coffee
French-style coffee
Gold Roast Freeze-dried
Ground Coffee
Instant coffee granules
Instant medium roast granules
Instant rich roast decaffeinated granules
Instant rich roast granules
Italian-style coffee
Medium roast granules
Mild blend
Organic Coffee
Organic dark roast coffee
Organic espresso blend
Organic instant freeze-dried coffee
Roast and Ground Decaffeinated Coffee
Roast and Ground Coffee

## DRIED FRUIT

Dates
Dried apricots
Dried banana
Dried mango
Mixed dried fruit
Raisins
Sultanas

## FRESH FRUIT & VEGETABLES

Apples
Avocados
Bananas
Clementines
Coconut
Grapefruit
Grapes
Lemons
Limes
Mangoes
Oranges
Pears
Peppers
Pineapples
Plums
Satsumas

## HERBAL TEAS

Chamomile
Citrus Zest Tea
Fairtrade Peppermint Tea
Fennel Liquorice Tea Bags
Green with Echinacea
Green with Ginseng Tea
Lemongrass
Lemon Valerian Tea Bags
Organic Masala Rooibos Tea
Organic Mint Green Tea Bags
Organic Rooibos Honeybush Buchu Blend Teabags
Organic Rooibos Tea
Raspberry Chilli Tea
Rosehip Hibiscus Tea Bags
Thyme
Wild Rooibos Tea

## HERBS AND SPICES

Basil
Black peppercorns
Chamomile

Cinnamon sticks
Cloves
Cracked pepper
Dill
Four-colour peppercorns
Ground black pepper
Ground cinnamon
Ground ginger
Ground mixed spice
Ground white pepper
Lemongrass
Mace
Mint
Mixed spice
Mulled wine spice mix
Nutmeg
Nutmeg powder
Oregano
Parsley
Rosemary
Peppermint
Sliced ginger
Tumeric powder
White peppercorns
Vanilla Extract Intense
Vanilla pods

## HONEY

Blossom honey
Clear honey
Forest honey
Pure clear honey
Set honey

Woodland honey – clear
Woodland honey – set
Cane syrup
Golden syrup

## ICE CREAM

Organic Belgian chocolate ice
   cream
Organic chocolate ice cream
Organic coffee ice cream
Organic vanilla ice cream
Vanilla ice cream
Vanilla toffee crunch ice cream

## JAM, PRESERVES, CHUTNEYS, AND SAUCES

Apricot and fig conserve
Apricot conserve
Apricot conserve with Fairtrade
   sugar
Bittersweet orange marmalade
   with cranberries
Blackcurrant conserve
Blueberry conserve
Blood orange marmalade
Chocolate hazelnut spread
Damson and sloe gin conserve
Fresh Elsanta strawberry
   conserve
Fresh raspberry and blackberry
   conserve
Hazelnut spread

Hedgerow conserve
Mandarin marmalade
Mango chutney
Morello cherry conserve with
   Fairtrade sugar
No-peel marmalade
Organic apricot conserve with
   Fairtrade sugar
Organic raspberry conserve with
   Fairtrade sugar
Organic strawberry conserve
   with Fairtrade sugar
Raspberry conserve
Red cherry conserve
Rhubarb and ginger conserve
Ruby red grapefruit marmalade
Seville orange marmalade
Seville orange marmalade with
   Kenmore whisky
Strawberry and pink champagne
   conserve
Strawberry conserve
Strawberry jam

## JUICES

Apple juice
Apple and mango juice
Apple and raspberry juice
Chilled orange juice
Orange juice
Orange and mango juice
Orange with carrot juice
Pineapple juice

Pure orange juice
Pure apple juice
Spiced apple juice
Tropical fruit juice
Tropical juice

## MUESLI
Apricot and Cranberry Muesli
Fruit and Nut Muesli
Tropical Muesli
Vine Fruit Muesli

## NUTS
Brazil nuts
Cashew nuts
Oven roasted and salted mixed
   nuts
Peanut butter crunchy
Peanut butter smooth
Roasted and salted brazil nuts
Roasted peanuts
Salted peanuts
Whole nut mix
Nut oils
Organic Amazon Flame Brazil
   Nut Oil

## RICE
Chocolate-coated mini rice
   cakes
Chocolate-coated rice cakes
Easy cook long-grain rice
Easy cook long-grain Thai white rice

Long-grain Thai white rice
Organic basmati rice
Organic brown basmati rice
Organic brown Jasmine rice
Organic fragrant Thai rice
Organic Thai Jasmine brown rice
Organic Thai Jasmine white rice
Organic thin slice rice cakes no
   added salt
Organic white basmati rice
Organic white Jasmine rice
Premium long-grain rice
Rich chocolate and crispy rice
   bar
Rice cakes very lightly salted

## SPIRITS
Chocolate liqueur
Coffee liqueur
White rum

## SUGAR
Cane sugar
Cinnamon Sugar
Dark Muscovado Sugar
Demerara Sugar
Golden granulated sugar
Granulated sugar
Lavender Sugar
Lemon Sugar
Light Muscovado Sugar
Organic Invert Sugar
Organic natural cane sugar

Organic raw cane sugar
Rose Sugar
Soft brown sugar
Vanilla Sugar
White granulated sugar
White sugar

## TEA
Assam
Breakfast tea
Ceylon
Darjeeling
Decaffeinated tea
Earl Grey
Kenyan
Oolong
White tea

## WINE
Ginger wine
Mead wine
Red wine
Rosé wine
White wine

## YOGHURT
Greek-style Yoghurt and Honey

# FAIRTRADE EVERY DAY – IDEAS FROM THE FAIRTRADE FOUNDATION

## Breakfast with the family

Wake up with juices from Cuba, single-origin coffee from Central America, Tanzania, or Ethiopia, and tea from Sri Lanka, India, and Uganda. Enjoy spreads and jams made with Fairtrade certified sugar from Malawi and Paraguay, or chocolate spreads and honey from Chile, Mexico, and Zambia. Fairtrade muesli is made with dried pineapples, apricots, and bananas, and brazil nuts, flavoured with cinnamon.

## Picnic in the park

Make a salad with Fairtrade rice from India and Thailand, avocados from Mexico and South Africa, grapes from South Africa and Egypt, oranges from Brazil and Morocco, and lychees from Mozambique. Try pears, plums, and apples from South Africa, or a smoothie with Fairtrade yoghurt and Fairtrade fruit from South Africa, Brazil, Peru, and Ecuador. For a vitamin boost, chew on dried apricots from Pakistan, dried mangoes from Burkina Faso, and dried pineapples from Costa Rica and Ghana.

## Healthy snacks

Snack on Fairtrade brazil nuts and peanuts from Bolivia and Malawi or cashew nuts from Burkino Faso, Mozambique, India, and El Salvador. Treat yourself to a delicious Fairtrade cake made with sugar and cocoa for chocolate heaven, or bananas and honey for an indulgent baked banana loaf. Feast on Fairtrade tropical fruit including bananas from the Windward Islands, Colombia, and the Dominican Republic, mangoes from South Africa, Brazil, Peru, and Ecuador, coconuts from St Vincent and Dominica, lemons and limes from South Africa, pineapples from Costa Rica and Ghana, and avocados from Mexico and South Africa.

## Dinner party with friends

Decorate the table with colourful Fairtrade flowers from Kenya. Enhance your main course with Fairtrade pepper, ginger, turmeric, and cinnamon from Sri Lanka. Or try nutmeg and vanilla from Uganda. Zest up fish and chicken dishes with lemons and limes from South Africa. Enjoy it all with a glass of Fairtrade red, white, or rosé wine from Chile, Argentina, and South Africa. For dessert you could bake a pineapple tarte tatin using Fairtrade sugar and pineapples, and top off the evening with a coffee liqueur made with Fairtrade rum or a herbal tea, and a cheeky Fairtrade chocolate mint or truffle.

While you are shopping responsibly, why not also consider choosing organic, free-range, and sustainable sources (especially fish and prawns) for your everyday ingredients?

# USEFUL ADDRESSES

Most major retailers and large stores nationwide stock a variety of Fairtrade fruits, teas, and coffees. Fairtrade certified ingredients and products are available in the following outlets:

## SUPERMARKETS

Asda   www.asda.co.uk
cocoa / honey / oils and pastes / spices / rice / wine

Booths   www.booths-supermarkets.co.uk
cocoa / spices

Booths Wines www.booths-wines.co.uk
wine

Budgens www.budgens.co.uk
dried fruits / honey / sugar

G. Baldwin & Co www.baldwins.co.uk
dried fruits / rice

Co-op   www.co-operative.co.uk
chutneys and preserves (chutney, sauces) / honey / nuts / spices / sugar / wine

Iceland   www.iceland.co.uk
chutneys and preserves (jams)

Marks and Spencer www.marksandspencer.com
chutneys and preserves (conserves, marmalades) / cocoa / honey / nuts / sugar / wine

Morrisons www.morrisons.co.uk
chutneys and preserves (conserves, marmalades) / cocoa / honey / nuts / spices / wine

Nisa Today's www.nisatodaysfoodstores.com
wine

Sainsbury's www.sainsburys.co.uk or www.sainsburystoyou.com
chutneys and preserves (jams, marmalades) / peppers / cocoa / honey / quinoa / spices / sugar / rice / wine

Somerfield www.somerfield.co.uk
wine

SPAR (UK) www.spar.co.uk
dried fruits / nuts / wine

Tesco www.tesco.com
chutneys and preserves (chutney, conserves, jams) / cocoa / dried fruits / honey / nuts / oils and pastes / spices / sugar / wine

Waitrose / Ocado
(www.waitrose.com or www.ocado.com)
chutneys and preserves (conserves, marmalades) / cocoa / herbs and spices / honey / rice / sugar / wine

# OTHER OUTLETS

Products listed include the main range of Fairtrade products currently stocked by these outlets.

Oxfam GB  www.oxfam.org.uk/shop
chocolates / cocoa / coffee / dried fruits / nuts / sugar / sweets

Thresher Group  www.threshergroup.com
wine

Earth Matters (Scotland)
www.earthmatters.co.uk
chutneys and preserves (chutney, jams) / cocoa / dried fruits / honey / nuts / oils and pastes

Just Fairtrade (The Midlands) www.jft.freeola.com
dried fruits / honey / sugar

Canterbury Wholefoods
www.canterbury-wholefoods.co.uk
chutneys and preserves (chutney, marmalades) / honey / oils and pastes / sugar

Sust! Milton Keynes Fairtrade Shop
www.sustmk.co.uk
chutneys and preserves (jams) / dried fruits / honey / rice

Infinity Foods Retail  www.infinityfoods.co.uk
dried fruts / nuts / quinoa / rice / seeds

The Fair Trade Shop Southampton
www.thefairtradeshop.org.uk
chutneys and preserves (chutney, jams, marmalades) / cocoa / dried fruits / honey / nuts / oils and pastes / quinoa / rice / sugar

Who Cares  www.whocares.gb.com/store
chutneys and preserves (jams) / dried fruits / spices / sugar

mondomundi (Channel Irelands)
www.mondomundi.com
cocoa / rice / spices / sugar

Ethics Girls  www.ethicsgirls.co.uk
chutneys and preserves (jams, marmalades) / cocoa / dried fruits / honey / nuts / oils and pastes / quinoa / spices / rice / sugar / wine

Ethical Shopper  www.ethicalshopper.co.uk
chutneys and preserves (jams, marmalades) / cocoa / dried fruits / honey / nuts / oils and pastes / rice / sugar

Ethicalsuperstore.com
www.ethicalsuperstore.com
chutneys and preserves (jams, marmalades) / cocoa / dried fruits / honey / nuts / oils and pastes / quinoa / rice / spices / sugar / wine

everywine.co.uk  www.everywine.co.uk
wine

FairlyGoods Shop www.fairlygoods.co.uk/shop
chutneys and preserves (jams, marmalades) /
cocoa / dried fruits / honey / nuts / oils and
pastes / rice / sugar

fairtrade boutique
www.fairtradeboutique.co.uk
nuts / oils and pastes / spices / sugar

GoodnessDirect www.goodnessdirect.co.uk
cocoa / dried fruits / honey / nuts / oils and
pastes / quinoa / spices / sugar

Greenline www.greenol.co.uk
cocoa / dried fruits / nuts / quinoa / quinoa flakes
/ rice / seeds / sugar

Simplyfair www.simplyfair.co.uk
chutneys and preserves (chutney, jams,
marmalades) / herbs and spices / nuts / oils and
pastes / rice

SLICE INNOVATIONS
www.sliceinnovations.co.uk/shop
chutneys and preserves (jams, marmalades) /
dried fruits / honey / nuts / oils and pastes / rice /
sugar

Steenbergs Organic Pepper and Spice
www.steenbergs.co.uk
lavender sugar / rose petals

The Ethical Food Company
www.ethicalfoods.co.uk
cocoa / honey / spices / sugar

Traidcraftshop www.traidcraftshop.com
chocolate / chutneys and preserves (conserves,
jam, marmalade) /coffee / dried fruits / herbs and
spices / honey / nuts / oils and pastes / quinoa /
rice / sugar / tea / wine

winedirect.co.uk www.winedirect.co.uk
wine

Whole Foods www.wholefoodsmarket.com/UK/
wine

## USEFUL WEBSITES

**The British Association for Fair Trade Shops**
A network of independent fair trade shops across
the UK
www.bafts.org.uk

**Ethical Directory**
A screened directory of green and ethically run UK
websites
www.ethicaldirectory.co.uk

# INDEX

# ACKNOWLEDGMENTS

### The Fairtrade Foundation

The Fairtrade Foundation would like to thank the following people for contributing to the wonderful selection of recipes in this book. All of the Fairtrade supporters that entered a recipe for the competition and those that held cook-offs to choose their best recipe; Conrad James from St Lucia and the other farmers and workers from Malawi, India, Uganda, the Dominican Republic, and Cuba who have taken time to share their lives through interviews and pictures; our celebrity supporters including Allegra McEvedy, Adjoa Andoh, Natasha Kaplinsky, Sir Steve Redgrave, Joanne Harris, Rose Gray and Ruth Rogers, George Alagiah, Oz Clarke, Hugh Fearnley-Whittingstall, Antony Worrall Thompson, Sheherazade Goldsmith, and Noel McMeel. We'd like to give particular thanks to Dawn Henderson, Serena Stent, and the team at Dorling Kindersley who have enabled this fantastic book to be published, and in particular to Caroline Gibson and Mary-Clare Jerram for approaching the Fairtrade Foundation with their exciting initial ideas for collaborating on a recipe book.

### Dorling Kindersley

Dorling Kindersley would like to thank all of the contributors to the competition and all of the celebrities who contributed recipes. Special thanks go to the judges, Sophie Grigson, Sarah Randell, and Eileen Maybin for bringing their expertise to bear in so many different ways. Thanks also to Sue Robinson, Editor of Sainsbury's *Magazine* and to the fantastic recipe testers who worked on the book – from Sainsbury's and from Not Just Food. Also thanks to Angela Nilsen for sifting through the competition entries to create a shortlist, to Megan Brady, the photographer's assistant, and to Hilary Bird for the index.

The recipe on page 98 was originally published in *River Café Pocket Books: Puddings, Cakes and Ice Creams*, 2006, Ebury Press

The recipe on page 126 by Allegra McEvedy is taken from the forthcoming *Leon Cookbook*, to be published in 2008 by Conran Octopus.

The recipe on page 142 was originally published in *The River Cottage Fish Book* by Hugh Fearnley-Whittingstall and Nick Fisher (Bloomsbury Publishing Ltd, 2007), and is reproduced here by permission of Bloomsbury Publishing Ltd and Greene & Heaton Ltd.

### Picture Credits

The publisher would like to thank the following for their kind permission to reproduce their photographs:
**Alamy Images**: Mark Boulton 15; Simon Rawles 80, 148, 200; **Fairtrade Media**: David Boucherie 36; Guzelian: Lorne Campbell 46; **The Fairtrade Foundation**: 14, 16, 44, 48, 54, 60, 98, 126, 131, 135, 138, 142, 151, 152; Sue Atkinson 13, 17, 18, 21; Marcus Lyons 210-211; Twin: 130
**Jacket images**: Back Flaps: **Alamy Images**: Simon Rawles
All other images © Dorling Kindersley
For further information see: www.dkimages.com